100 Best Solitaire Games

100 Best Solitaire Games

Sloane Lee & Gabriel Packard

CARDOZA PUBLISHING

ABOUT THE PUBLISHER

Cardoza Publishing is the foremost gaming and gambling publisher in the world with a library of over 100 up-to-date and easy-to-read books and strategies. These authoritative works are written by the top experts in their fields and with more than seven million books in print, represent the best-selling and most popular gaming books anywhere.

FIRST EDITION

Library of Congress Catalogue Card No: 2003109496
ISBN: 1-58042-115-6

Illustrations by Dora Storch

Visit our web site (www.cardozapub.com) or write for a full list of books, advanced strategies and computer games.

CARDOZA PUBLISHING

P.O. Box 1500, Cooper Station, New York, NY 10276
Phone 1-800-577-WINS
email: cardozapub@aol.com

For E. Smith and G. Ingram

ACKNOWLEDGEMENTS

Real big thanks to: Avery Cardoza, Eli Brag and Lowell Packard.
Also, salut encore une fois l'equipe francaise.

TABLE OF CONTENTS

INTRODUCTION

Most people know one or two solitaire games, but there are actually well over 1,000 out there. This book brings you the best 100 and teaches you how to play them using easy, step-by-step instructions and clear diagrams. You'll also find advice and strategy tips to help you fine-tune your solitaire skills and get the most out of every game.

There are games that you'll need strategy to win, games that are just plain fun to play, classic games, new games, and travel games. They're all neatly organized, so you can find exactly what you're looking for, instantly.

You'll find all of the essential classic games, along with the most popular modern ones.

Travel Solitaire Games

Solitaire is the perfect game for playing while you're on the move—car journeys, flights, even the bus or train. The problem with many solitaire games, though, is that they take up a lot of space. Unless you've got a private jet or limousine, space is one thing you generally don't have a lot of when you're getting from A to B. This is why we have developed an exclusive range of travel solitaire games. They don't require much space and are perfect for whiling away the hours as you're on your travels. Look out for the "✈" symbol which marks these games.

Computer Solitaire Games: *Freecell, Solitaire*

If you play *FreeCell* or *Solitaire* on your computer, you should enjoy the chapter on computer solitaire games. It shows you variations of these computer classics and gives you playing tips on how to play better and win more.

If you don't play solitaire on a computer—or if you don't even have a computer—don't worry. This book shows you how to play the popular computer solitaire games that everybody's talking about. And all you need is a regular pack of cards.

THE BASICS OF SOLITAIRE

The Two Main Types of Solitaire Games

There are two main types of solitaire games. In one type, strategy games, you build all the cards onto the foundation. And in the other, fun games, you aim to get rid of all the cards.

Strategy Games

Building is the main part of these games. You aim to build all of the cards somewhere, usually the foundation. Most strategy games follow this general pattern:

1. Prepare the cards: Take the jokers out of the pack. Then shuffle it.

2. Set up the cards: You'll usually deal out several columns of cards for the base and maybe a few more cards as a reserve. In some games, you take cards out of the pack before you start dealing and place them in the foundation.

3. Play the game: The aim will usually be to build all of the cards onto the foundation. To do this, you'll need to shift the cards around the base, usually by building cards from one part of the base to another. This allows you to free up cards you need for the foundation. There may be a reserve. This supplies cards that you can use for building. Most games involve you dealing cards from the stock. These cards are available for you to use for building.

4. Redeal: When you've dealt all of the cards from the stock, or when you've become completely stuck, you may be allowed one or more redeals. This means that you collect up certain cards, and deal them again.

5. End the game: The game ends when you have either won, by building all of the cards onto the foundation, or lost because you cannot make any more moves.

Fun Games

The aim of these games is simple: get rid of all your cards. Most of the fun games follow this pattern:

1. Prepare the cards: Make sure you've taken the jokers out of the pack and shuffled it.

2. Set up the cards: This may involve dealing out a few piles of cards, or cards in a grid. Some games don't have any set up at all.

3. Play the game: The aim is to get rid of all your cards. You often do this by matching up pairs of cards—two cards of the same rank or suit—and discarding them together. The rules may say that the pair must be next to each other or a certain distance apart. Sometimes you'll discard cards that add up to a certain amount. If that amount is 10, for example, you can get rid of a 6 with a 4, or an 8 with a 2.

4. Redeal: You may be allowed one or more redeals.

5. End the game: If you discard all the cards, you win. If you become stuck and can't make any more moves, you don't win.

When we call these "fun" games we're not saying that the other games aren't fun. They are. We just mean that these games don't require too much thinking. If you want to stretch your mind, pick a strategy game. But if you want to relax, unwind and give your brain a rest, a fun game is the perfect way to do so.

A Guided Tour of Places in a Solitaire Game

There are only five places a card can go in a game of solitaire: the foundation, the base, the reserve, the stock pile and the wastepile.

Base, Reserve: Playing solitaire is like doing a jigsaw puzzle. The cards are like the pieces of the puzzle. You have to sort them out and put them together in the correct way to make the picture. Usually, the foundation is like the place where you put the pieces together. And the base and reserve are like the place where you sort the pieces out.

The base is also known as the *tableau*, but to keep things simple this book will always use the word *base*.

Foundation: The foundation is the final destination for cards. If there is a foundation in the game, the aim will be to move all of the cards into it. You'll have to move them in a particular order, depending on which game you're playing.

Once you've moved a card to the foundation you're not allowed to move it again— it must stay put. But as soon as a card is in the foundation, you are allowed to build on it.

Stock pile: To set up the game, you have to deal out a number of cards. After you've done this, you'll usually still have some cards left over. These are called the stock pile. Sometimes it's just called the stock. During the game you'll end up dealing these cards, often onto the base or **wastepile**.

Wastepile: This is where you put the cards that won't fit anywhere else. Sometimes you deal cards from the stock pile onto the wastepile to see if you can move them somewhere else. Not all games have a wastepile.

CHAPTER I
THE MOST POPULAR
SOLITAIRE GAMES

In this chapter we teach you how to play the two most popular games in the world: *FreeCell* and *Klondike*, which is often just called *Solitaire*. Why are they so popular? Well, the main reason is that you can find them preinstalled on virtually every computer in the world. Also, *Klondike* has long been a popular solitaire game, even before the rise of IBM, Windows, Bill Gates and spam. So if you know just one solitaire game, there's a good chance that it's *Klondike*.

Don't worry if you've never played solitaire on a computer. Just go through this chapter as you would any other. All of the games are fully explained. You'll find everything you need, right here.

I. FREECELL

Because you can find it on virtually every computer on earth, *FreeCell* has also become one of the world's favorite ways of avoiding work.

Whether you're playing it on your computer, or playing with a pack of cards; whether you're playing in you free time, or when you should be writing a report for your boss, you're sure to enjoy this modern classic.

To set up, you put all the cards in the base. This means you don't have any dealing during the game. What you do have, however, is the use of four "FreeCells." Think of the FreeCells as storehouses. You can put cards from the base into the FreeCells, keep them there as long as you like, and then move them back to the base or on to the foundation.

If you're careful, you can win *FreeCell* almost every time you play.

Game type: Strategy
Aim: Build all of the cards onto the foundation
One game takes about: 20 minutes
Expect to win this game: Usually
Packs of cards: One

Set Up

Deal eight columns of seven cards and four columns of six cards.

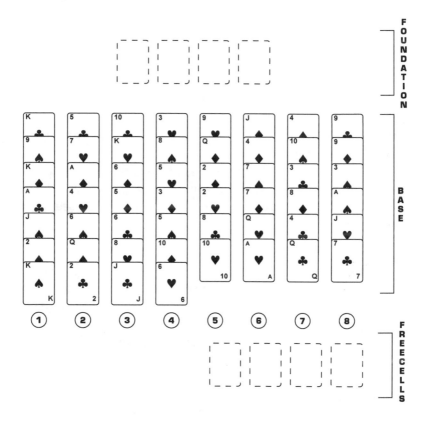

How To Win

Free up the aces, move them to the foundation and build them up in suit to kings.

How To Play

The top card of each column is available for play. You can move any of these available cards into one of three places:

1. Directly onto the foundation

2. Elsewhere on the base—build down in alternating color on any other top card

3. Into an empty FreeCell

Use the four FreeCells as temporary storehouses. You can move any available card into an empty FreeCell. All cards in the FreeCells are available and you may use them to build onto the foundation or the base.

When you create a gap in the base by moving all of the cards out of one column, you have two options. You may keep the gap open for as long as you like or, if you want, fill it straight away. When you do fill a gap, do so with any available card.

Redeals

There are no redeals in this game.

Advice

☞ To win, you must think long term. It's tempting to fill up the FreeCells to help you free an ace or some other card, but you usually shouldn't do it. Try not to clog up the FreeCells for any reason. Keep as many of them open as possible.

☞ Try to move a card to a FreeCell only if you think you'll be able to move it out again soon. The more FreeCells open, the more room to maneuver. The more room to maneuver, the easier it is to free up the cards you need.

☞ At the start of the game, you should look to see where the aces and other cards are. Then, work out the best way to free them without locking the FreeCells.

☞ A useful strategy is to focus on one or two cards, and plan a way of freeing it that will leave most of the FreeCells available when you've done so. That way, you won't have to think too far ahead.

☞ When you have a gap in the base, it is useful to build a series of cards in it. The more cards the better. When cards are in sequence, they generally won't block the game. This is because no high cards are trapping lower cards underneath themselves.

☞ You should try also to create gaps in the base. These are even more useful than open FreeCells because they can hold a number of cards. FreeCells, on the other hand, hold just one card each. You can move a sequence of cards into a gap by using a sneaky little move called a run. To learn how, read on.

☞ The run is a useful move for FreeCell and many other building games. It lets you move a sequence of cards—J-10-9-8, for example—into a gap or from one pile to another. Here's an example to show you how it works. Let's say that, half way through a game, you have all of your FreeCells open, and two of your columns look like this:

STEP 1

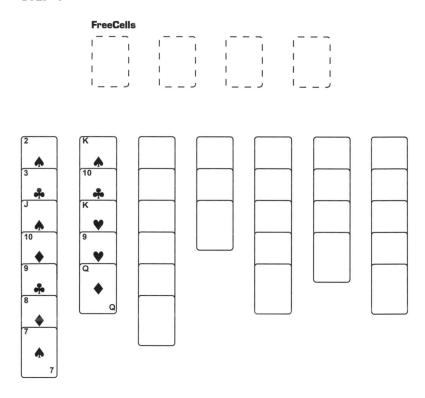

☞ You want to move the J♠, 10♦, 9♣, 8♦ and 7♠ from the left hand column to the Q♦ on the right. You can use a run to move all five cards and end up with all your FreeCells clear. This is how. First, you move the 7♠, 8♦, 9♣ and 10♦ to the four FreeCells. Then you build the J♠ onto the Q♦. Then simply build the four cards from the FreeCells onto the jack. And bingo! You moved all five cards in one swift operation. That's the beauty of the run.

STEP 2

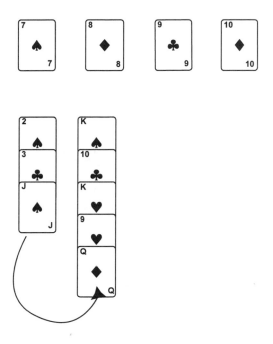

STEP 3

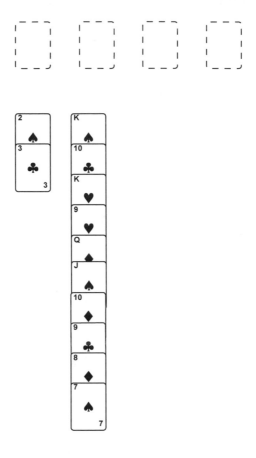

☞ In a run, the cards you move must already be in sequence. The number of cards you can move depends on how many gaps and FreeCells you have available. As a rule, you take the total number of gaps and empty FreeCells, add one, and the number you're left with will be the number of cards you can move.

2. BONUS FREECELL

If you like chocolate cake, you probably like chocolate brownies and Mississippi mud pie, too. Following this logic we're going to introduce you to some other games in the *FreeCell* family. They're all similar to the original, but all of them have something different to offer. *Bonus FreeCell*, for example, has eight FreeCells instead of four.

Game type: Strategy
Aim: Build all of the cards onto the foundation
One game takes about: 15 minutes
Expect to win this game: Usually
Packs of cards: One

Play exactly as you would a regular game of *FreeCell*, but set up the cards in the following way. Deal eight columns, each containing six cards. This is the base. Now, deal four cards below the columns.

In *Bonus FreeCell*, you have eight FreeCells to use instead of just four in regular *FreeCell*. Four of them are already filled when you start the game.

There is just one other difference between this game and regular *FreeCell:* you may only fill gaps in the base using kings.

3. HARD CELL

This is *FreeCell's* tough cousin. Its key difference from the original is in the set up. You have to deal some of the cards face down. This makes the game harder because, unlike regular *FreeCell*, you don't know the position of every card. You are, however, allowed to turn the face-down cards face up during the game. This useful feature allows people without x-ray vision to play.

Game type: Strategy
Aim: Build all of the cards onto the foundation
One game takes about: 17 minutes
Expect to win this game: Usually
Packs of cards: One

Play following all the rules of *FreeCell*, but when you set up the game, place all of the cards face down. When you've finished setting up, turn the top four cards of each column face up.

From then on, play as normal. Whenever you uncover a face-down card, turn it face up. When it's face up, it's available for play.

4. JAIL CELL
This is a cross between *Bonus FreeCell* and *Hard Cell*.

Game type: Strategy
Aim: Build all of the cards onto the foundation
One game takes about: 20 minutes
Expect to win this game: Usually
Packs of cards: One

Play exactly the same as *Bonus FreeCell*, except when you're setting up, deal all of the cards face down. When you've finished dealing, turn the top four cards of each pile face up.

Whenever you uncover a face down card during the game, turn it face up. It becomes available for play.

Remember, there are eight FreeCells in this game.

5. STALACTITES
This is a trickier version of *FreeCell*.

Game type: Strategy
Aim: Build all of the cards onto the foundation
One game takes about: 12 minutes
Expect to win this game: Sometimes
Packs of cards: One

Set Up
Deal a row of four cards. Place them sideways. They are the foundation. Below, deal the rest of the cards in eight columns of six cards each.

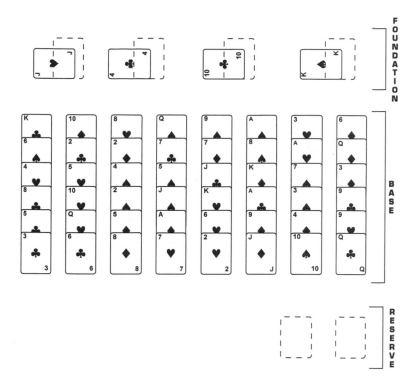

How To Win

To win, you must build up the four foundation piles so they each have thirteen cards in them. You should build regardless of suit.

How To Play

After you've set up the cards, you must decide how you are going to build on the foundation. You can either build up in ones (4-5-6-7-8, etc.) or you can build up in twos (4-6-8-10-Q-A-3, etc). Whichever way you choose, you must build all four of the foundation piles in that way. Don't worry about suit or color when building on the foundation—just build up in sequence.

When you're building on the foundation, place cards the normal way up. But make sure you keep the first four foundation cards turned sideways. This makes it easy to see when you've got thirteen cards in a foundation pile. For example, if your first card is the 4♣, you'll know to stop building on that pile when you lay down a 3. It doesn't matter if you're building up in ones or twos, you'll always stop when you hit 3.

The rule to know when to stop building, as you've probably worked out, is this: stop building when you get to the card that is one rank below your first foundation card.

Remember that in this game the sequence of cards continues in a big loop, just like this: 10-J-Q-K-A-2-3-4-5-6-7-8-9-10-J-Q, and so on. You get the idea—an ace is both high, above a king, and low, below a two. This is called continuous sequence. It allows you to build thirteen cards onto each foundation pile, no matter what the first card is.

Once you've decided how you're going to build, you can start moving cards. The top card of each base pile is available for play.

You aren't allowed to move cards around the base from one column to another; you can only move them to the foundation or reserve. The reserve has two spaces, and we'll explain how it works by comparing it to a motel.

House Rules of the Reserve Motel

Think of the reserve as a kind of motel—cards can stay there on their way to the foundation, but they have to follow a few house rules.

Rule 1: Any available card can stay in The Reserve, so long as there is space.

Rule 2: The Reserve only has two rooms, so a maximum of two cards can stay there at any one time.

Rule 3: Once a card has checked in to The Reserve, it cannot return to the base. Instead it must move on to the foundation.

Okay, let's see how this all fits together by going through an example. First of all, have a look at the diagram above.

Let's say we've decided to build the foundation up in ones. We could move the J♦ on to the 10♣ in the foundation. Then we could move the Q♣ on top of that J♦. Now we can't move any more cards from the base directly onto the foundation because none of them fit. So we need either a queen to go on the J♥; a 5 to go on the 4♣; a king to go on the Q♣; or an ace to go on the K♠. None of these required cards, however, are on the top of any of the piles.

This is where the reserve comes into play.

Say we want to build on the K♠ and we've decided to free up the A♦ from Column 4 to build on it. To free A♦ we move the 7♥ into one of the reserve spaces. This puts A♦ on the top of Column 4, and once it's on the top we can move it on to the K♠ in the foundation.

Redeals

There are no redeals in this game.

Advice

☞ There is more flexibility here than in *FreeCell* because you have eight spaces in the reserve instead of four—the four FreeCells act like a reserve. Even so, you should still try keep as many of those spaces open as you can. Whenever possible, only move a card to the reserve when you know you can send it on to the foundation soon after. The cards that are safe to move will depend on which cards you dealt into the foundation. These change each game.

☞ Think ahead. If you are aiming to free up a card, work out how many cards you'll need to move to the reserve and how long they're likely to sit there. The fewer cards and the shorter time, the better the move. That should serve you as a general guideline rather than a set-in-stone rule.

6. MIX AND MATCH

Mix and Match is a variation of *Stalactites*. It gives you a bit more flexibility in playing.

Game type: Strategy
Aim: Build all of the cards onto the foundation
One game takes about: 12 minutes
Expect to win this game: Sometimes
Packs of cards: One

This is played exactly the same as *Stalactites*, except for one difference. In *Mix and Match* you can, if you want, build some of the foundation piles up in ones and others up in twos. For example, you could build three foundation piles up in twos and the other up in ones.

There is a handy way to remember which foundation piles are going up in ones and which are going up in two. On the piles you're building up in ones, place the cards on the left hand side of the first foundation card. And on those you're building up in twos, build on the right.

7. KLONDIKE (often called SOLITAIRE)

Klondike is probably the most popular solitaire game of all time. Even before it was put on to virtually every computer in the world, it was a favorite. There are many ways to play *Klondike* and it has many variations. On most computers, you'll find this version, usually under the name *Solitaire*.

You're aiming to move all the cards onto the foundation. It may sound easy, but often the cards you need will be trapped. To free them, you'll have to build cards from one base column to another.

Game type: Strategy
Aim: Build all of the cards onto the foundation
One game takes about: 5 minutes
Expect to win this game: Sometimes
Packs of cards: One

Set Up

Deal seven columns to form the base. Overlap the cards in each column. In the first column there should be one card; in the second column, two cards; in the third, three cards; and so on. There should be seven cards in the seventh column.

The top card of each column should be face up, and all of the other cards should be face down. You will have quite a few cards left over—they form the stock.

You'll end up with something that looks like this:

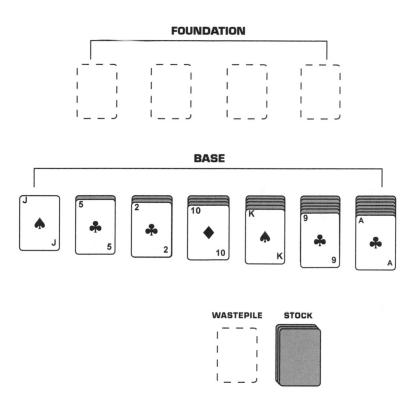

How To Win

When the aces become available, you should move them to the foundation and build them in suit up to kings. If you get all of the cards to the foundation, you win.

How To Play

The top card of each column is available for play. You can either build it onto the foundation or to a different column on the base. When you build on the base, build down in alternating colors. You can put a black 9 on a red 10, for example.

Each time you uncover a face-down card on the base, turn it face up. Once the card is face up, it becomes the new top card of that pile. The top card, remember, is always available for play.

When you've built a number of cards onto a column in the base, you can, if you want, move them around the base in a group. This is how.

Before you make your move, you can group the top card with one or more of the cards built in sequence underneath it. You can move as many or as few as you like, as long as they are built in sequence, are on the top of a pile, and have somewhere to go.

Keep the cards in sequence when you move them. You still have to build down in sequence, so make sure that the bottom card of your group is one rank lower than the top card of the pile you're building onto. Also, make sure it's the opposite color.

Let's look at an example of moving cards in a group to see how it works. Let's say that on the top of one column you have two cards built in sequence, 9♣ on the 10♦. You can move them both in a group onto a black jack, the J♠, for example. The two cards will stay in the same sequence. So after the move, you'll end up with 9♣ on 10♦ on J♠.

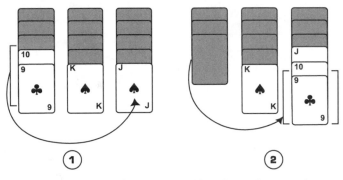

You may only build in a group, like this, when you're moving cards around the base, from one column to another. It doesn't work for building cards onto the foundation.

If you create a gap in the base by moving away all of the cards from one of the seven columns, you may only fill it with a king. Any available king will do.

The top card of each foundation pile is available for play onto the base. This is quite unusual for a solitaire game. Usually you aren't allowed to move cards out of the foundation.

Deal the stock into a wastepile in sets of three cards. Form each set of three cards into a fan on the top of the wastepile. The cards in the fan count as the top three cards of the wastepile. As you use each card, the one underneath becomes the new top card and is available for play.

After each set of three cards, pause, make all the moves you want to, and then deal another set of three.

If you don't use some of the cards in a fan, just square them up and leave them on the top of the wastepile. Deal the next fan of three directly on top of them.

Redeals

When you've dealt all of the cards from the stock, pick up the wastepile and turn it over. It becomes your new stock. Now you should redeal and play as normal.

You may redeal as many times as you want.

Advice

☞ Get all the cards turned face up as soon as you can. You can't free up a card if you don't know where it is. Knowledge is power.

☞ Just because you *can* move a card, doesn't mean you should. Here is a useful guideline to bear in mind: Don't move 3's to the foundation until all the aces are already there. Don't move 4's until all the 2's are there. Don't move 9's until all the 7's are in place, and so forth.

☞ As soon as you start the game, deal out your first three cards from the stock. This will give you a few extra points.

☞ If a king is blocking lower cards in a column, move it into a gap as soon as you can. It's often a bad idea to take a king out of the wastepile. You won't be able to move it to the foundation until very late in the game. And until then it will just take up a valuable gap.

☞ All gaps are valuable. It's sometimes worth making several moves to create one.

☞ Before you make any move, ask yourself, What's in it for me? Don't make any move just because you can. Only do it if there's something to gain. If it will let you bring a card from the wastepile into the base, for example, or if it will create a gap, it's usually worth doing. Remember, if you don't move a card from one base column to another now, you can always do so later.

☞ If you have the choice, keep cards in the same suit together when you're building on the base. This makes it easier to unload them to the foundation later. Don't go out of your way to keep the suits together, though. Only do it if you have the option easily available.

8. "KLASSIC" KLONDIKE

Here is another much-played version of *Klondike*.

Category: Strategy
Aim: Build all of the cards onto the foundation
One game takes about: 5 minutes
Expect to win this game: Sometimes
Packs of cards: One

Play as a regular game of *Klondike*, but make the following changes:

1. Deal cards from the stock one at a time, not in groups of three.

2. When moving cards around the base, from one column to another, follow this rule. If the cards on top of a column are in sequence, you must move them together as a group. If there are no cards in sequence, on top of a column, you should just move the top card on its own.

3. Once you move a card to the foundation, it stays there. The top cards of the foundation piles are not available for play.

4. You are not allowed any redeals.

Advice

☞ Try to remember which cards have gone into the wastepile. It's useful to know where cards are. You don't get any redeals in this game, so the cards won't come around again. If you want to get a card at the bottom of the wastepile, you have to dig it out.

☞ When you start the game, deal just one card from the stock into the wastepile. This will give you an extra option, and it might give you something useful to work with.

9. AGNES

If variety is the spice of life, *Agnes* gives you two spoonfuls. As well as being a variation of *Klondike,* this game is different almost every time you play it.

In regular *Klondike,* the cards you build on in the foundation are always aces. Not so here. These foundation cards are chosen at random near the start of each game.

Agnes has a reserve. This also gives the game a different flavor than *Klondike,* which doesn't have one.

Game type: Strategy
Aim: Build all of the cards onto the foundation
One game takes about: 7 minutes
Expect to win this game: Often
Packs of cards: One

Set Up

Deal twenty-eight cards into seven piles, as you would in *Klondike.* Then in the foundation, deal one card. This is the first foundation card and should be face up. It's an important card because it decides the rank of the foundation for the duration of the game. If that first foundation card is 9♥, for example, the rank of the foundation will be 9. So you'd put the other 9s into the foundation row when they become available.

Once you've dealt that single card, deal a row of seven cards below the foundation. This is the reserve. You can move cards from the reserve onto the base or directly onto the foundation.

How To Win

After you've moved your foundation cards to the foundation, you should build each of them up in suit until its pile contains thirteen cards.

If your first foundation card is a 9, then you'll finish each pile with an 8. You'll always finish the foundation pile one rank below the first foundation card.

How To Play

This part of the game starts out the same as *Klondike*, too. You build down on the base in alternating colors, and you build up in suit on the foundation.

But there are some key differences:

1. When you get a gap in the base, you may fill it with any card that is one rank lower than that first foundation card you dealt. In our example the first foundation card was 9♥, so you would fill gaps with 8s.

2. When you can't make any more moves, don't deal the stock into a wastepile as you would with *Klondike*. Instead, deal the cards in batches of seven onto the reserve: put one card on each of the seven piles.

3. The top card of each reserve pile is available for play. You will have enough cards for three deals of seven onto the reserve pile. After these three deals, you'll have two cards left over. When you get stuck for the fourth time, deal these two cards face up next to the reserve row. You may use them as you would use any other reserve cards.

4. If you get any gaps in the reserve, you may only fill them by dealing the next layer of reserve cards.

5. When you're building up, you may always follow a king with an ace, and an ace with a two. And when you're building down, you may follow a two with an ace, and an ace with a king. This is called continuous ranking.

Redeals

There are no redeals allowed in this game.

Advice

☞ After you've set up the game, take a minute to look at the base. Work out which cards you'll need soon and which cards you won't need until later. This will depend on the first foundation card. If it is a 9, for example, you'll need the other 9s, and the 10s and jacks soon. But you won't need the 7s and 8s near until the end.

☞ Gaps in the base are useful, so you might want to work to create them. But gaps in the reserve don't help you at all.

10. LIFEBOAT

This version of *Klondike* is bigger, lasts longer, and is more flexible than the original. The reason for these upgrades is simple: you use two packs of cards instead of one.

In *Lifeboat*, as in *Klondike*, you build up on the aces. But because you're using two packs, there are eight aces instead of four. You also deal out more piles on the base, so there is more room for moving cards around.

Category: Strategy
Aim: Build all of the cards onto the foundation
One game takes about: 10 minutes
Expect to win this game: Sometimes
Packs of cards: Two

How To Play

Play as you would a regular game of *Klondike*, except make the following changes:

1. Use two packs of cards shuffled together.
2. Instead of dealing seven piles in the base, deal eleven. As with regular *Klondike*, the first pile will contain one card; the second pile, two cards; the third, three; and so on. The eleventh pile will contain eleven cards. Deal all of these cards face down, and then turn the top card of each pile face up.

How To Win

Move all eight aces to the foundation and build them up all up in suit to kings.

Redeals

You are not allowed any redeals in this game.

11. SPIDERETTE

What happens when you take the foundation out of *Klondike?* You end up with *Spiderette.*

That's what makes *Spiderette* an unusual game: there is no foundation, so you do all your building right on the base.

Game type: Strategy
Aim: Build all of the cards onto the foundation
One game takes about: 10 minutes
Expect to win this game: Sometimes
Packs of cards: One

Set Up

Deal the cards as you would for a game of *Klondike.*

How To Win

To win, you have to build all of the cards in suit from king down to ace. You must build the cards into four of the columns on the base—each containing all thirteen cards of one suit.

How To Play

The top card of each column is available for play elsewhere on the base. Build down regardless of suit.

Once two or more cards of the same suit are in sequence at the top of the base column, you may move all of those cards together as a set.

You are aiming, remember, to get all thirteen cards of a suit in sequence. Once you have this on the top of a column, you're allowed to take all thirteen of those cards off the base.

You can fill gaps in the base with any available card or with any group of cards in sequence. But you don't have to fill gaps straight away.

When you can't make any more moves—or you have made all of the moves that you want to—you should deal out seven more cards from the stock. Put one card face up on the top of each column in the base. You must fill all gaps before you deal.

After you've dealt these seven cards, continue playing as normal. When you get stuck again, deal seven more. Then repeat this process one more time. You'll now have three cards left over; when you get stuck for the third time, deal these three cards onto the first three columns.

Redeals

You're not allowed any redeals.

Advice

☞ Although you don't have to build in suit on the base, it is a good idea to do so. In order to win the game, you have to build all of the cards *in suit* from king down to ace. So it pays to build in suit whenever you can.

CHAPTER II
STRATEGY GAMES

12. FLOWER GARDEN

This is one of the most playable and addictive solitaire games you'll ever find. Don't say we didn't warn you.

In the set up you, deal all of the cards into the base and reserve, so there is no dealing during the game. The key to doing well with *Flower Garden* is learning when to use cards from the reserve and when to save them for later.

There is a fair chance of winning, but to do so you'll have to use your head and work out the best order for freeing up the cards.

Game type: Strategy
Aim: Build all of the cards onto the foundation
One game takes about: 20 minutes
Expect to win this game: Sometimes
Packs of cards: One

Set Up

Deal six overlapping columns of six cards. Below, spread out the remaining cards in a large fan.

How To Win

When the aces become available, move them to the foundation and build them up in suit to kings.

How To Play

The top card of each base column is available for play, as are all of the cards in the reserve. A card in the middle of the reserve is still available and you can pick it up and move it.

You can move any of the available cards directly onto the foundation or use them to build on the base. When you're building on the base, build down regardless of suit or color on the top card of any column.

In the base, you may fill gaps with any available card.

Redeals

You're not allowed any redeals.

Advice

☞ Don't move cards from the reserve to the base unless you absolutely have to. This allows you to keep the maximum number of cards in play throughout the game.

☞ Try to free up the aces, 2s and 3s as soon as you can.

☞ There is a handy little trick to help you keep track of the cards that you're trying to free up. Simply turn them sideways in their columns. This lets you see at a glance exactly where they all are. You'll usually be looking for the next card to go on each of the four foundation piles, so you may like to have one card of each suit turned sideways.

13. FLOWER BED

This variation of *Flower Garden* is easier to win than the original and requires less strategy. It's a good one to play if you like *Flower Garden* but want to win more often or if you don't want to think so hard, or both.

Game type: Strategy
Aim: Build all of the cards onto the foundation
One game takes about: 20 minutes
Expect to win this game: Sometimes
Packs of cards: One

Play exactly the same as a game of *Flower Garden,* except for one difference: In the set up, deal seven rows of five, not six rows of six.

14. GOLF

The wastepile is the sun around which this whole game orbits. And to win the game, guess where all the cards must be. That's right—the wastepile.

But you can't just toss any old card on there. Instead, you have to build on it. When you're building on the wastepile, you're allowed to build up, then down, then down again, then up again. In fact, you can stop and change directions as often as you like.

So put on your golf shoes, dust off your clubs—and diamonds, spades and hearts—and get ready to tee off.

Game type: Strategy
Aim: Build all of the cards onto the foundation
One game takes about: 5 Minutes
Expect to win this game: Rarely
Packs of cards: One

Set Up

Deal five overlapping columns, each containing seven cards. Then deal one card into the wastepile.

How To Win

To win, you must build all of the cards from the base onto the wastepile. It is very difficult to achieve this, so you should aim to leave the smallest possible number of cards on the base.

How To Play

The top card of each base column is available for play onto the wastepile only. You can't build onto other columns on the base.

On the wastepile, build up or down regardless of suit. When you're building, you can switch direction as often as you like, building up, then down, then up again. For example, you could build on the 10♣ in the following way:

10♣; J♥ (up); 10♦ (down); 9♠ (down); 8♣ (down); 9♥ (up).

Deal one card from the stock onto the wastepile.

On aces, you are only allowed to build 2s. You *may not* build a king onto an ace.

A king in this game is like a lost ball in a real game of golf—it draws things to a halt. If you get a king on the top of the wastepile —either by building it onto a queen or by dealing it from the stock—you're not allowed to build any card on top of it. Instead you have to deal a card from the stock and place it on top of the king.

Redeals

There are no redeals allowed in this game.

Advice

☞ Don't rush. Before you make any move, work out exactly which other moves it will lead to. The more moves, the better. You should aim to move the maximum number of cards off the base between each card dealt from the stock.

☞ Some cards are more difficult to discard than others, so you must be careful what you do with them. There are two groups of tricky cards: kings and queens is the first; and aces and 2s is the second. We'll deal with each in turn.

☞ The only way to discard a king is with a queen. So you must save your queens for this purpose.

☞ At the start of the game, count the kings and queens in the base. If you are lucky, some of the kings will be in the stock. This may mean you have an extra queen or two to play with. If you are unlucky, there will be more kings than queens on the base. If this happens, the game is still winnable; you'll just have to wait for the queens to show up on the stock pile.

☞ Similarly, the only way to get rid of an ace is with a 2. So you should conserve your 2s in the same way that you should conserve queens.

☞ To a lesser extent, jacks are also key cards. They are the only ones that can lead queens to the wastepile. Use them wisely and try to conserve them for queens.

☞ It is very difficult to win outright, so you should aim instead to leave.

15. BISLEY

You want options? We'll give you options. There are eight different piles you can build cards on in this game's foundation. Not one, not two, not five, but eight. Yes, eight whole piles. That's because you put all the kings and aces into the foundation and build on them: up on the aces, down on the kings.

On the base you may both build up and down, switching directions as often as you like on any of the piles.

Game type: Strategy
Aim: Build all of the cards onto the foundation
One game takes about: 8 minutes
Expect to win this game: Often
Packs of cards: One

Set Up

Take the four aces out of the pack and put them in a row. They are the first four foundation piles. Later in the game, you'll put the kings in the foundation too, and they'll form the other four piles. There's no need to worry about that now, though. Let's get back to setting up the game.

Underneath those aces, deal out the rest of the cards in thirteen overlapping columns. First, deal four overlapping columns of three cards each. Then to the right of them, deal nine overlapping columns each containing four cards.

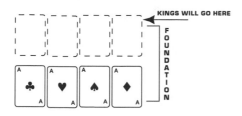

How To Play

The top card of each column is in play. You may move these top cards onto the foundation or elsewhere on the base. When you're building on the base, build in suit, either up or down, on the top card of any other column. You're allowed to build in different directions on the same column. For example, you could build the 7♦ on top of the 6♦. Or you could instead build the 6♦ on top of the 7♦.

You're not allowed to build an ace onto a king or a king onto an ace.

As soon as the kings are free, place them into the foundation. Put the K♠ above the A♠, the K♥ above the A♥, and the other kings above the aces of the same suit.

You may start building on aces immediately and on kings as soon as they are in the foundation. Build down in suit on the kings, and build up in suit on the aces.

If you remove all of the cards from a column and make a gap, you're not allowed to fill it. The column simply disappears.

How To Win

As soon as the kings become available, move them to the foundation. Build in suit on the foundation – build up on the aces and down on kings. You win the game when you have built all of the cards onto the foundation. It doesn't matter how many of each suit are on the king and how many are on the ace. As long as all the cards are on the foundation, you win.

Redeals

In this game, you're not allowed any redeals.

Advice

☞ Move the kings to the foundation as early as possible. The sooner they are there, the sooner you can start building on them.

☞ Build cards onto the foundation whenever you can. There is no advantage in keeping cards on the base.

☞ As far as possible, never build card down on a column that already contains a lower card of the same suit. For example, if a column has 5♣ in it, you should try to avoid building any club ranked 6 or higher on that column. Doing so will trap the lower card.

☞ Similarly, you should try to avoid building a card up on a column that already contains a higher card of the same suit.

16. SCORPION

This game has a twist in its tail. But, you'll be glad to hear, it's a good twist. When you get completely stuck, there are three cards in the reserve that you can use to give the game a little jump-start. Another notable feature is that *Scorpion* has no foundation, so you build on the base.

Game type: Strategy
Aim: Build all of the cards onto the foundation
One game takes about: 10 Minutes
Expect to win this game: Sometimes
Packs of cards: One

Set Up

Deal seven overlapping columns, each containing seven cards. In the first three columns deal the three bottom cards face down and the top four face up. And in the remaining three columns, deal all of the cards face up.

You'll have the three cards left over. Deal them face down below the base; they form the reserve.

How To Win

There is no foundation in this game. So you do all your building on the base. To win, you must get the cards into just four piles—one for each suit. At the bottom of each pile you should have a king. And that king should be built down in suit to ace.

How To Play

You can build down in suit on the top card of any pile. This is quite a normal way of building. But the selection of cards available for building is more unusual. You can use any face up card from the base to build with, even if it is covered by other cards or at the bottom of a pile. If other cards cover the card you want to move, you simply move all of them together as one unit keeping all cards in the correct order.

Whenever you uncover a face down card you turn it face up and it becomes available for play.

If you create a gap in the base by moving all of the cards away from a column, you may only fill that gap with a king. If there are cards covering the king that you use, then you must move them as well.

You may not build on an ace.

If you get completely stuck and can't make any more moves, you are allowed to break out the emergency rations in the reserve. To do this, deal the three reserve cards face up onto the first three columns. If you get stuck again, the game is over.

Redeals

You're not allowed any redeals.

Advice

☞ Your first priority should be to uncover the face-down cards in the base.

☞ If you can't find a card you're looking for, it will be one of the face-down cards.

☞ When you get a gap, carefully choose which king you can put there—you can only fill gaps with kings, remember. See which card will be exposed when you move the king, and then trace which other cards you can move on top of the newly exposed one.

☞ You should be aware that certain orders of cards are impossible to unravel and will block the game. For example, 9♠, 8♠, 10♠. You'll never be able to move the 8 onto the 9 because the 10 blocks it. You'll never be able to move the 10 because the 8 blocks the 9. Be careful not to accidentally build this kind of order while you are moving cards around.

17. BAKER'S DOZEN

As the American people declared in 1776, kings can be very annoying. In politics they can raise taxes and pass laws, and in solitaire they can trap the cards that you need in the base. *Baker's Dozen* is a game that recognizes this and lets you do something about it. At the start of the game, you get to put kings to the bottom of piles and underneath cards that they might be trapping. You might think of it as a mini solitaire revolution.

Game type: Strategy
Aim: Build all of the cards onto the foundation
One game takes about: 10 minutes
Expect to win this game: Often
Packs of cards: One

Set Up

Deal thirteen overlapping columns of four cards each. When you've done this, go through each column looking for kings:

1. If a king is on the top of any column, move it to the bottom.

2. If there is a king on top of any other cards of its own suit, then put that king under those cards.

3. If you get two or three kings in the same column, put them all to the bottom, but keep them in order.

How To Win

To win, you must free up the aces, move them to the foundation and build them up in suit to kings.

How To Play

The top card of each column is available for play onto the foundation or elsewhere on the base. On the base, build down regardless of the suit on the top card of any other column. For example, you could move 3♠ onto 4♠ because 4 is one rank higher than 3.

You're not allowed to fill gaps in the base.

Redeals

There are no redeals allowed in this game.

Advice

☞ You should aim to uncover low cards trapped under high cards of the same suit.

☞ If you have an available card that can go onto the foundation, don't move it there straight away. First, check to see whether it might be useful in the effort to free up other low cards trapped under high cards of the same suit.

☞ Whenever you can, build down in suit on the base. This makes it easier to transfer the cards to the foundation later.

☞ Try to build the four foundation piles simultaneously —don't rush one ahead of the others.

18. HAMLET

If you like the strategy and brainpower that *Baker's Dozen* requires, and if you like your games to last a long time, this variation is for you. It uses two packs of cards, so it's bigger and lasts longer. A winning combination, if ever there was one.

Game type: Strategy
Aim: Build all of the cards onto the foundation
One game takes about: 18 minutes
Expect to win this game: Often
Packs of cards: Two

Play using the same rules as *Baker's Dozen*, but use two packs of cards shuffled together. Deal thirteen columns of eight cards, and aim to build all eight of the aces up in suit to kings.

19. GOOD MEASURE

When a butterfly beats its wings in Dorchester, says Chaos Theory, it might one day cause a hurricane in Brooklyn. Small changes can have large effects and everything is connected.

This game appears very similar to *Baker's Dozen*, but just a couple of small changes in the set up make it quite different. So batten down the hatches, shuffle the cards and read on.

Game type: Strategy
Aim: Build all of the cards onto the foundation
One game takes about: 8 minutes
Expect to win this game: Often
Packs of cards: One

You play following the same rules as *Baker's Dozen*, but you set up the cards a bit differently. Before you start dealing the cards, take any two aces out of the pack and place them in the foundation row. Then deal ten columns of five cards instead of thirteen columns of four. As with *Baker's Dozen*, you should check for kings before you start playing. Move all of the kings to the bottom of their columns and underneath other cards of the same suit in the same column.

20. VOLCANO

Here is another variation of *Baker's Dozen*. Again, a bit of tinkering makes this game's engine run differently.

Game type: Strategy
Aim: Build all of the cards onto the foundation
One game takes about: 8 minutes
Expect to win this game: Often
Packs of cards: One

Play in the same way as *Baker's Dozen* except for two differences:

I. Aim to move the aces *and* the kings to the foundation. Build the aces up in suit and build the kings down in suit. To win the game, you must build all of the cards onto the foundation. It doesn't matter how many go onto the king piles and how many go to the ace piles.

2. On the base, build up or down regardless of suit. If you want to, you may switch directions, building both up and down on the same column.

21. BETSY ROSS

Concentration, that's what you need to play this game. There are four foundation piles, and you need to build each of them using a different pattern. On top of that, there is no base, so you deal cards straight from the stock to the wastepile. It's useful to keep an eye on which cards you've dealt. Stay focused, and you'll do just fine.

Game type: Strategy
Aim: Build all of the cards onto the foundation
One game takes about: 5 minutes
Expect to win this game: Sometimes
Packs of cards: One

Set Up

Take any ace, 2, 3, and 4 out of the pack and put them in a row. These cards will serve as signposts to remind you how to build on the row below. Where is the row below? You're just about to deal it. Take any 2, 4, 6, and 8 out of the pack, and put them in another row under the first. These are the four cards that you will build onto. You should end up with something that looks like this:

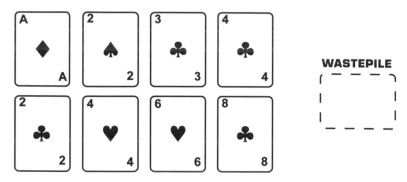

How To Win

Build up all of the cards onto the bottom row. You must build in the correct order, which we'll explain in a moment. If you win, each pile will contain thirteen cards and will have a king on top.

How To Play

You have to build the cards onto the four piles in the bottom row, that's the one with the 2, 4, 6 and 8. You have to build on each of them in a different way.

As we mentioned earlier, the cards in the top row—A, 2, 3, 4—are there to remind you how to build on each pile. The four patterns, as you'll see, are very simple:

On the **2**, build up normally, in ones. That's why there's an ace above it.
2-3-4-5-6-7-8-9-10-J-Q-K

On the **4**, build up in twos. Hence the 2.
4-6-8-10-Q-A-3-5-7-9-J-K

On the **6**, build up in threes. That explains the 3.
6-9-Q-2-5-8-J-A-4-7-10-K

On the **8**, build up in fours. Which makes sense of the 4 above it.
8-Q-3-7-J-2-6-10-A-5-9-K

Build up regardless of suit on all four of the piles. Throughout this game, the suits of the cards don't matter. All you have to worry about is rank.

You should also know that in this game the picture cards and aces have the following values:

king =13   queen=12   jack=11   ace=1

Now that you know the building patterns and how much each card is worth, deal the cards from the stock pile one at a time.

If you can build a card onto one of the four piles, do so. If you can't, put it face up on the wastepile. The top card of the wastepile is always in play. That means you can build it onto one of the four piles in the foundation. If you do use the top card of the wastepile, the card underneath is uncovered and this becomes the new top card.

Redeals

When you have turned over all of the cards in the stock, you can pick up the wastepile, turn it over and deal those cards again. This is how you redeal in *Betsy Ross*. You're allowed to do it twice.

Advice

☞ You should spread out the cards in the wastepile as you deal them. This lets you keep track of where everything is.

☞ Look out for "reversed sequences" in the stock pile, they can keep you from winning unless you tackle them early on. An example of a reversed sequence is 6,5,7. Why is it a bad thing? Well, you won't be able to build on the 6 because the 5 doesn't appear until afterward. But by the time it does appear, the 6 is already gone—trapped under the 5. Then when the 7 shows up, there is no 6 for it to go on. Of course, in *Betsy Ross* you don't always build up in ones, so reversed sequences won't always block you. But they can.

☞ You may get less obvious reversed sequences for the piles that you build up in twos, threes and fours. For example, a 4, 2, 6 would be a reversed sequence for the pile you build up in twos.

22. OLD GLORY

This version of *Betsy Ross* allows you to play with the maximum amount of strategy.

Game type: Strategy
Aim: Build all of the cards onto the foundation
One game takes about: 8 minutes
Expect to win this game: Sometimes
Packs of cards: One

Play as you would a game of *Betsy Ross*, except for one difference: Instead of dealing out the cards one by one, spread the entire stock pile out in front of you. Keep the cards in the correct order and play them one at a time either to the foundation or to the wastepile. You must play the cards in the same order that they are in the stock pile.

23. DUCHESS

It's all or nothing in this game. When you're moving cards around the base, you have to move the entire row. There are no half-measures. You can't move one card, or a small group of cards. You've got to go the whole nine yards.

On top of that unusual feature, this classic build-up-the-foundation game has a little of everything—there are fans, a reserve, a base, a stock pile, a wastepile, a foundation, a redeal. Boy, this is almost like reading the glossary, isn't it?

Game type: Strategy
Aim: Build all of the cards onto the foundation
One game takes about: 8 Minutes
Expect to win this game: Sometimes
Packs of cards: One

Set Up

First, form the reserve by dealing four fans, each containing three cards. Leave a space for the foundation, and underneath that space deal a row of four cards, the base.

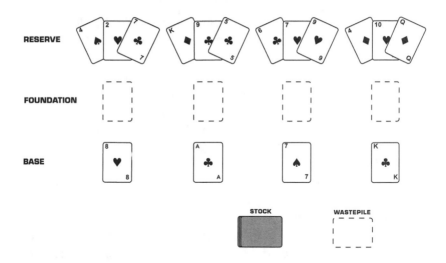

How To Win

To win, you must build all of the cards up in suit onto the foundation.

How To Play

First, look at those four fans in the reserve. Choose the top card of any of them to be the first foundation. In our example, you could choose 7♣, 5♣, 9♥ or 10♥. As soon as you've chosen your card and moved it to the foundation, you may start building on it. Build up and in suit.

When the other three cards of the same rank become available, put them in the foundation also. Let's say with our example that we chose 7♣ to go into the foundation. That means as the other three sevens become available, we'd put them in those other three foundation spaces and then build on them.

After you've chosen and moved that first card, the main part of the game starts. From now on, the top card of each fan is always available for play and so is the top card of each of the four rows in the base.

As well as building up in suit on the foundation, you can also build on the base. When building on the base, you should build down in alternating color on the top card of any row. So, in our example we could build the Q♦ onto the K♣.

When you're building on the base you may always build an

ace on a 2, and a king on an ace. And when you're building on the foundation you're allowed to build an ace on a two, and a king on an ace.

If you want to build cards on the base from one row to another, you must move the entire row as one unit. No matter how many cards are in the row, you have to move them all together as one. The bottom card of this row must fit onto the top card of the row you're moving it to.

If you create a gap in the base by moving all of the cards away from one of the rows, you may fill it with any top card from the reserve. If there are no more cards in the reserve, use the top card of the wastepile.

Deal the cards from the stock pile one at a time into the wastepile. The top card of the wastepile is always available for play onto the foundation or the base. After dealing each card to the wastepile, pause and make any moves you can. All of the cards that were in play up until now are still in play. The game goes on as before, but with the new feature of dealing from the stock pile.

Redeals

You're allowed one redeal. When you have dealt the whole stock pile, pick up the wastepile and turn it over. It becomes the new stock pile; deal it out one card at a time and play as normal.

Advice

☞ Choose the first foundation card so that the cards in the reserve and base will help you build. If there is a 6 on top of one of the fans, for example, and there are other 6s in the reserve, then that is a good card to choose. This is because you should aim to get the first foundation cards in place as early as possible. The sooner they're in the foundation, the sooner you can start building on them.

24. LA BELLE LUCIE

If we were into bad jokes, we might be tempted to ask, Why is this game like Elvis Presley? The answer would be, Because they both have a lot of fans. Luckily for you, though, we shall avoid such drollery. Instead we'll tell you that this is a truly brilliant, very playable, totally engrossing game.

In most games, the base is made up of columns, here it's made of fans. When you get stuck you are allowed two redeals and a special bonus pick.

Game type: Strategy
Aim: Build all of the cards onto the foundation
One game takes about: 15 minutes
Expect to win this game: Sometimes
Packs of cards: One

Set Up

Deal the cards into seventeen fans; each fan will have three cards in it. You'll have one card left over—put this into a pile of its own and treat it just like another fan.

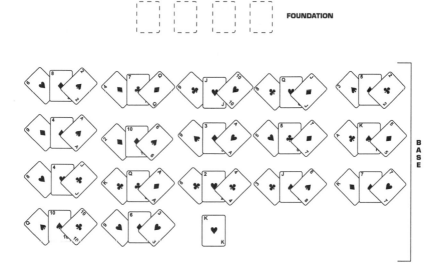

How To Win

To win, you must free up the aces, move all four of them to the foundation and build them up in suit to kings.

How To Play

The top card of each fan is available for play. You can move it to one of two places: the foundation, or the top card of any other fan. When building on other fans, build down in suit.

If you create a gap by removing all the cards from one fan, you are not allowed to fill it—the fan just disappears.

Redeals

When you can't make any more moves, collect up all the cards, shuffle them, and redeal them into as many fans of three as possible. If you have one or two cards left over at the end, put them into a fan of their own. You should treat this fan like any other.

You're allowed a total of two redeals.

Bonus

After your second redeal, you are allowed to take one card from anywhere in the base and build it either onto the foundation or elsewhere on the base. You can use this bonus move any time you want to, after the second redeal.

Advice

☞ You should always try to avoid moving the last card of a fan. Once that last card is gone, the fan vanishes—you can't fill the gap. Each time you loose a fan, you have fewer places to build cards. You want to keep the maximum number of places to build cards.

☞ Whenever you can, you should move cards to the foundation. There is no advantage in keeping them on the base. The only exception to this rule is when the card is the last one in a fan. When it is, you should only move the card to the foundation for one of two reasons: One, if you need the card on the foundation to overcome a block somewhere else on the base. Or two, if all of the other cards in the same rank are already on the foundation.

25. TREFOIL

This version of *La Belle Lucie* allows you to win more often.

Game type: Strategy
Aim: Build all of the cards onto the foundation
One game takes about: 15 minutes

Expect to win this game: Sometimes
Packs of cards: One

You play in exactly the same way as *La Belle Lucie*, but you set up the cards in a slightly different way. Before you deal, take the four aces out of the pack and put them in the foundation. Then deal the remaining cards into sixteen fans of three.

26. SHAMROCKS

With *Shamrocks*, a variation of *La Belle Lucie*, you get more *and* less freedom when you're building on the fans. On the one hand you are allowed to build both up and down on the same fan. But on the other, you aren't allowed to let a fan contain more than three cards.

Game type: Strategy
Aim: Build all of the cards onto the foundation
One game takes about: 15 minutes
Expect to win this game: Sometimes
Packs of cards: One

Set Up

Deal the cards in exactly the same way as you would for a game of *La Belle Lucie*.

How To Win

Free up the aces, move them to the foundation, and build them in suit up to kings.

How To Play

Play in the same way as *La Belle Lucie*, except for three differences:

1. After you've set up the cards, look for the four kings. Move each of them to the bottom of its fan.

2. When you're building on the base, you may build in sequence either up or down, as you wish. If you want to, you may build up *and* down on the same fan, switching direction as much as you like.

3. You're never allowed to have more than three cards in any fan.

Redeals

You're not allowed any redeals in this game.

Advice

☞ As with *La Belle Lucie,* you should always try to avoid moving the last card of a fan.

☞ Try not to build one foundation ahead of the others. Keep them level with one another.

27. PERSEVERANCE

When you redeal in this game, you redeal big. You don't just pick up a wastepile and turn it over. Here you pick up the whole base and deal it out again.

If you want to be well versed in solitaire, this good old-fashioned building game is essential to know. It's a classic.

Game type: Strategy
Aim: Build all of the cards onto the foundation
One game takes about: 10 minutes
Expect to win this game: Often
Packs of cards: One

Set Up

First, take the four aces out of the pack and put them into the foundation row.

Then deal out twelve columns of four cards each.

How To Win

Build the aces up in suit to kings.

How To Play

The top card of each column is available for play onto the foundation or elsewhere on the base. When you're building on the base, you have to build down in suit.

You're allowed to move groups of cards that are in sequence and on the top of a column. As long as the bottom card of such a group fits on the top card of another column, you can move the group as a single unit. So, if 7♦-6♦-5♦-4♦ are on the top of a column, you could move them as a unit onto the 8♦.

Redeals

When you can't make any more moves, you get to redeal. To redeal you should collect up the base piles, one by one. Start with the last pile you dealt and collect them in the reverse order to which you dealt them. Keep the cards in order within their piles, and don't shuffle them. When you've collected up all the piles into one big, new pile, use it to deal out as many columns of four as you can. If there are less than four cards left over at the end, deal them as a pile of three, two, or one, and play it as you would any other column. You are allowed two redeals.

Advice

☞ On the base, get as many cards in sequence as you can. When you redeal, they'll still be in sequence, for the most part. You want them in sequence because it makes them easier to build onto the foundation.

28. CALCULATION

Destiny isn't a matter of chance, it's a matter of choice, so the self-help wisdom goes. This is certainly true when you're playing *Calculation*, an important part of which is deciding where to put unplayable cards. There are four wastepiles to choose from. In fact, most of the strategy in this game comes from building cards onto the wastepiles in the best possible order—the order that will allow you to build them onto the foundation at a later stage in the game.

Game type: Strategy
Aim: Build all of the cards onto the foundation
One game takes about: 15 minutes
Expect to win this game: Sometimes
Packs of cards: One

Set Up
Take any ace, 2, 3 and 4 out of the pack and place them in a row. These four cards form the foundation.

How To Win
To win the game, you must build all of the cards onto the foundation, regardless of suit. There are four foundation piles, and you must build on each of them using a slightly different pattern.

On the **ace**, build up in the normal way:
Sequence: 2-3-4-5-6-7-8-9-10-J-Q-K
On the **2**, build up in twos:
Sequence: 4-6-8-10-Q-A-3-5-7-9-J-K
On the **3**, build up in threes:
Sequence: 6-9-Q-2-5-8-J-A-4-7-10-K
On the **4**, build up in fours:
Sequence: 8-Q-3-7-J-2-6-10-A-5-9-K

Remember, the suits of the cards don't matter in this game, only the rank is important.

If you win, each pile will contain thirteen cards and will have a king on top.

How To Play
Deal the cards from the stock pile one at a time. If you can put a card onto the foundation, do so. If you can't, put it in any of the four wastepiles. Any card can go onto any wastepile; there is no pattern to follow.

The top card of each wastepile is always available for play. That means you can move it to any of the foundation piles—as long as it fits, of course.

Keep the cards in each of your four wastepiles spread out. This lets you keep track of where the cards are. You'll need to know this to build the wastepiles in the best possible way.

Redeals
You're not allowed any redeals.

Advice

☞ Be careful which wastepile you put cards onto. You don't want to trap low cards, which you'll need early on, underneath high ones.

☞ The cardinal sin, when building on the wastepiles, is to put a card on top of a lower card of the same suit. If you do this, you won't be able to win the game.

☞ Save one of the wastepiles just for kings. This stops other cards from getting stuck underneath the kings, which are the very last cards in each sequence. If you get all four kings in one pile and you still have more cards to deal from the stock, you can put other cards on top of the kings. But wherever possible, never put a king on top of another card.

☞ Whenever you can, build cards onto the wastepile in the reverse order to which they have to go onto the foundation.

29. BRISTOL

In this game, think of yourself as the director of a construction company, The Solitaire Building Co. The four foundation piles are luxury hotels that you have to build. You build them from aces, the underground fitness studios, up to kings, the penthouse suites.

The base is your builder's yard where your construction workers prepare the construction materials—here you may build down. And the reserve is the builders' merchant where you buy everything you need. Even if you don't like this analogy, you should still like the game.

So, let's get to work. Time is money.

Game type: Strategy
Aim: Build all of the cards onto the foundation
One game takes about: 5 Minutes
Expect to win this game: Often
Packs of cards: One

Set Up

Deal eight fans, each containing three cards. These fans form the base. Underneath it, deal a row of three cards. This is the reserve.

How To Win

When the aces become available, move them to the foundation and build them up to kings, regardless of suit. All building in this game is regardless of suit.

How To Play

First, you should check the fans. If any of them have a king as the top card, move it to the bottom of the fan.

The top card of each fan is always available for play, and so is the top card of each reserve pile. You may build available cards onto the foundation or the base.

As the aces become available, move them to the foundation and build them up to kings, regardless of suit. On the base, you may build down—also regardless of suit—on the top card of any fan.

Deal cards from the stock, three at a time. Put one card on each of the three reserve piles. Then pause, make your moves, and deal three more cards to the reserve. Keep repeating this process until you have no more cards in the stock.

You're not allowed to fill gaps in the base. But if you have a gap in the reserve pile, you may fill it on your next deal from the stock.

Redeals

You're not allowed any redeals in this game.

Advice

☞ Seek out and move high cards that trap lower cards underneath them.

30. GRANDFATHER'S CLOCK

This is a classic building game with a twist: it is based on a clock face. The twelve foundation cards are arranged in a circle, and you build on them until they show the numbers on an actual clock. You build the pile at three o'clock, for example, until it has a 3 on top of it.

Game type: Strategy
Aim: Build all the cards onto the foundation

One game takes about: 10 minutes
Expect to win this game: Often
Packs of cards: One

Set Up

Take these cards out of the pack:
2♥, 3♠, 4♦, 5♣, 6♥, 7♠, 8♦, 9♣, 10♥, J♠, Q♦, K♣.

Now, arrange them, in order, in a circle with one card at each "number" of the clock face. Put the 2♥ at the "five o'clock" position and then work clockwise, putting 3♠ at "six o'clock," 4♦ at "7 o'clock," and so on.

Next, you should deal the remaining cards into eight columns, each with five cards in it. Make the cards overlap so you can see all of them. This is the base.

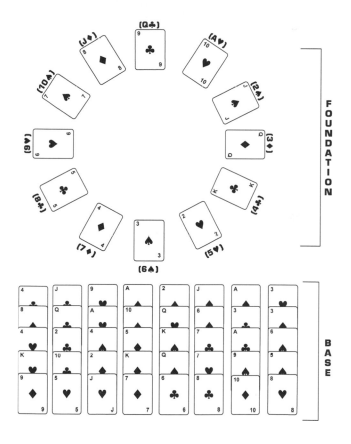

How To Win

The circle of cards is the foundation. You should think of it as a clock face. Build up the card at "1 o'clock" until the top card is an ace; build up the card at "2 o'clock" until you get a 2 on the top; build the "3 o'clock" card until you get a 3; and so on. Jack is "11 o'clock" and queen is "12 o'clock."

Look on the diagram. In brackets next to each card is the name of another card. This card named in brackets will be the last card of each pile. You should stop building on a pile when you reach the card named in brackets next to it.

How To Play

The top card of each column is available for play. You can move any top card to the foundation or onto the top card of any other column in the base. When you're building on the base, build down, regardless of suit or color.

You're allowed to fill gaps in the base with any available card.

Redeals

No redeals are allowed.

Advice

☞ Gaps are valuable. It's sometimes worth making several moves to create a gap.

☞ When you're building cards on the base, bear in mind which cards will go onto each foundation pile. Every card must go onto one of the twelve piles along with a few other cards. While cards are on the base, where possible you should try to group together the cards that will go onto any single foundation pile.

31. GREAT-GRANDFATHER'S CLOCK

This is a harder version of *Grandfather's Clock*. There are stricter rules about how you can build on the base, so you need to use more strategy to win.

Game type: Strategy
Aim: Build all the cards onto the foundation
One game takes about: 12 minutes
Expect to win this game: Sometimes
Packs of cards: One

Play exactly the same as *Grandfather's Clock*, except when you create a gap in the base, you may not fill it. Also, when building on the base, you may only build in alternating colors.

32. STRATEGY

This game is like a pension plan. It's all about building for the future.

Ultimately, in *Strategy*, you want to build all your cards onto the foundation. But there is no base, so you deal cards from the stock placing unplayable cards into a number of wastepiles—you choose which card goes to which wastepile.

The wastepiles are the key to the game. If you build your cards into the wastepiles the right way, you'll later be able to offload them to the foundation and win.

Game type: Strategy
Aim: Build all of the cards onto the foundation
One game takes about: 15 minutes
Expect to win this game: Sometimes
Packs of cards: One

How To Win

As the aces show up, place them into the foundation and build them up in suit to kings. To win, you must build all of the cards onto the foundation. You'll end up with thirteen cards in each of the four piles.

How To Play

Deal out every card in the pack, one at a time. If you can build a card onto the foundation, do so. If you can't, you'll have to put it onto any one of eight wastepiles. You're allowed to put any card onto any wastepile—you don't have to build or follow any pattern. The top card of each wastepile is always available for play onto the foundation.

Redeals

You're not allowed any redeals.

Advice

☞ The key to the game is building the wastepiles. Most of the strategy is in selecting the right pile for each card.

☞ Never place a card in a pile that already contains a lower card of the same suit.

☞ Try to put higher cards at the bottom of piles and build generally downward.

☞ Save one pile for kings. Once you've put all four kings into that pile, you are free to put any card on top. And once each king goes into the pile, you're free to put the queen of the same suit on top. Once the queen is down, you can add the jack of the same suit, and so on.

☞ Some people save two piles and mix kings and queens in both of them. If you do this, make sure you never put a king on top of a queen of the same suit.

☞ Where possible, don't start a pile with a low card. For the purpose of this game, anything 9 or under is low.

☞ Keep the cards in the piles spread out. That will allow you to see what is where. This should stop you from accidentally trapping low cards.

☞ An alternative way to play is to keep the piles all squared up, not spreading them out at all. This makes you rely on your memory. It adds an extra dimension of difficulty to the game. So if you want to increase the challenge, give it a try.

33. DOUBLE OR QUITS

In my end is my beginning, a famous poet once wrote. He probably wasn't thinking about solitaire when he penned the line, but it certainly applies to *Double or Quits*. What sets this game apart from the crowd is the unusual pattern in which you build the cards. We'll explain later how the pattern works.

The thing to remember here, though, is that the sequence just goes round and round in one continuous loop. You can start at any point and it's still the same sequence. As soon as you get to the end, you're at the beginning again.

Aside from that, the overall aim of the game should be quite familiar to you. You try to build all of the cards onto the foundation. There is no base, but there is a nice big reserve.

Game type: Strategy
Aim: Build all of the cards onto the foundation
One game takes about: 5 Minutes
Expect to win this game: Often
Packs of cards: One

Set Up

Deal eight cards face up. Place them in a square formation, with one card at each of the four corners and one card for each of the four edges. The bottom center card is the first foundation card, and the other seven cards are the reserve.

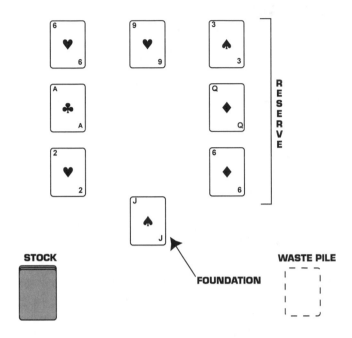

How To Win

Apart from kings, which you discard, build all of the cards onto the foundation in the following sequence:

A-2-4-8-3-6-Q-J-9-5-10-A-2-4-8-3-6-Q-J-9, and so on

Build regardless of suit.

When you play, you'll probably start the sequence somewhere in the middle. Where you start depends on the first foundation card—that's the card at the bottom center of the square. Whatever your starting point, the sequence is circular. So when you get to the end, you find yourself at the start again and you can just keep on building.

How To Play

All of the cards in the reserve are available for play onto the foundation. The foundation, remember, is whichever card you dealt during the set up into the bottom center position in the square.

In our example, it's a jack. So we'd look at the sequence, above, and see that the next card should be a 9. We have a 9 in the reserve—9♥—so we can build that onto the jack. And now the top card of the foundation is a 9, so we're looking for a 5.

When you remove a card from the reserve, fill the gap straight away with a card from the top of the wastepile. If there are no cards in the wastepile use a card from the stock.

Deal the cards from the stock one at a time onto the wastepile. The top card of the wastepile is always available for play onto the foundation.

If you come across a king at any stage, discard it. And if, when setting up the cards, you find you have a king in the reserve or as the first card of the foundation, discard that king and replace it using a card from the stock.

Redeals

You're allowed two redeals. When you have dealt all of the stock cards into the wastepile, turn over the wastepile and use it as a new stock pile. Deal the cards one by one and play as normal.

Advice

☞ The sequence you use in this game is quite rare. It takes a bit of getting used to. As you play, you should start to learn the order. You need to know the order to plan which moves to make, and memorizing it makes everything quicker.

☞ When you have a card in the reserve that you can move to the foundation, don't move it straight away. Instead, you should wait until the top card of the wastepile is one that you want to use soon. Only then should you move the card from the reserve. This will allow you to draw useful cards out of the wastepile and save them. And it will also prevent you from clogging up the reserve with cards that you won't be able to move until late in the game.

What is that sequence all about?

The clue to answer this question is in the name of the game, *Double or Quits*. Each card in the sequence is double the value of the card that comes before it. So ace, which has a value of 1, doubled is 2; 2 doubled is 4; 4 doubled is 8.

Now, we know what you're thinking here: Hang on, buster—8 doubled is 16, and there ain't no 16 of diamonds. Rest assured, there is a simple explanation. This is it. When you double your card and end up with a number greater than 13, you simply subtract 13 from that number. So when you double 8 and get 16, just subtract 13, and bingo—you're left with 3. Remember that jacks = 11, and queens = 12.

It's easy when you know how.

34. LITTLE SPIDER

Like soccer games, bikinis, and Korea, this game is divided into two parts. In both parts of *Little Spider* you can build on the foundation. But when you start the game there is no base. So during the first part, you have to create the base. Then in the second part you get to shift cards around the base from one pile to another.

There you have it: one game, two parts. As Shakespeare might have said, two-parting is such sweet sorrow, that we might play this game until tomorrow.

Game type: Building
Aim: Build all of the cards onto the foundation
One game takes about: 25 minutes
Expect to win this game: Often
Packs of cards: One

Set Up

Deal two rows of four cards. These make up the base. Leave a space for the foundation between the rows, like this:

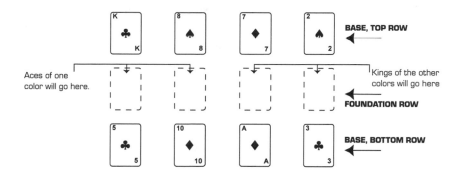

How To Win

As they become available, move four cards to the foundation: two kings of one color and two aces of the other.

You can choose either two red kings and two black aces, or two black kings and two red aces. Either way, each of these four cards must be of a different suit.

Build the two kings *down* in suit to aces. And build the two aces *up* in suit to kings.

How To Play

There are two parts to this game. We'll go through them one at a time.

Part 1, During The Deal

Deal all of the cards onto the base in sets of eight—four on the top row and four on the bottom.

After each set of eight, take a break from dealing and move whatever cards you can onto the foundation. On the base, the top card of each pile is available for play.

Continue dealing the cards in sets of eight. Eventually you'll have four cards left over in the stock. That's not enough for a set of eight, of course. So just put these last four cards on the top row, one on each pile.

Make all the moves you can, and then move on to part two of the game.

Part 2, After The Deal

The top card of each pile is still available for play onto the foundation. But now, you can also move available cards elsewhere on the base. When you're building on the base, build on the top card of any pile, and build up or down regardless of suit.

You're not allowed to fill gaps in the base.

Redeals

There are no redeals in this game.

Advice

☞ The best strategy is to keep the cards on the base for as long as possible, build them in suit and then transfer them to the foundation later—as late in the game as possible.

☞ Although you don't have to, it is useful to build in suit on the base. When you do this, you should build in the opposite direction to the way the suit is going on the foundation. That may sound tricky, but it's not. Use this guide to check which way you should aim to build on the base:

If you have these cards in your **foundation**...
Black kings and red aces K♠, K♣, A♥, A♦

...you *have to* build this way on the **foundation**...
Build spades and clubs down, and build hearts and diamonds up

...and you should *aim to* build this way on you **base.**
Build spades and clubs up, and build hearts and diamonds down

If you have these cards in your **foundation**...
Red kings and black aces K♥, K♦, A♠, A♣

...you *have to* build this way on the **foundation**...
Build spades and clubs up, and build hearts and diamonds down

...and you should *aim to* build this way on you **base.**
Build spades and clubs down, and build hearts and diamonds up

35. YUKON

You know what's really annoying? When you're playing a building game and there's a card you need for the foundation but you can't get to it because it's buried in the base. Well, guess what. In this game you're allowed to move *any* card from anywhere in the base. You'll never get stuck again, right? Well, not exactly.

It may sound easy, but there are a few other rules to keep you on your toes and stop the game being too easy.

Game type: Strategy
Aim: Build all of the cards onto the foundation
One game takes about: 10 minutes
Expect to win this game: Often
Packs of cards: One

Set Up

Deal seven piles of face down cards.

- In Pile 1, on the far left, there should be one card.
- In Pile 2, there should be two cards.
- In Pile 3, there should be three cards.

Keep adding one more card to each successive pile until you get to Pile 7, which should contain seven cards and should be on the far right.

Now turn the top card of each pile face up.

When you've made up those seven piles, deal an overlapping column of four face up cards on Piles 2 through 7. You'll get a set up that looks like this:

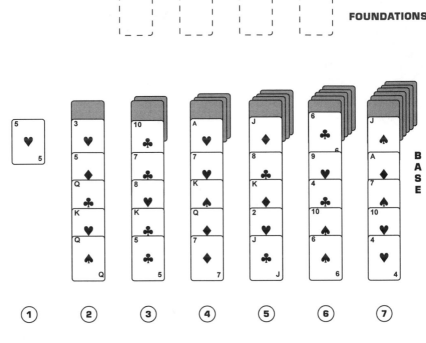

FOUNDATIONS

BASE

How To Win

Free up the aces, move them to the foundation and build them in suit up to kings.

How To Play

In this game, there are two different ways to build. One way for building onto the foundation, and another for building on the base.

You build on the foundation in quite a standard way, using the top card of any base pile.

When building from one base pile to another, however, you use quite an unusual method. You can move *any face-up card*, no matter where it is in the pile. Pretty handy, isn't it? If you move a face-up card that has other cards on top of it, then you move the card with all of those other cards as well. Think of them all stuck together as one unit.

When you're building on the base, you must build the bottom card of the group you're moving onto the top card of any other pile. And you must build down in alternating colors.

There are just three more things you need to know to play this game.

First, when you uncover a face-down card, turn it face up. You can now play it like any other face-up card. If you uncover a pile of face-down cards, turn just the top one face up.

Second, you can only fill gaps in the base with kings. Remember, if your king has other cards on it, you must move all of the cards together.

And third, as soon as an ace becomes available, you must move it to the foundation.

That's all. Now deal those cards out, and start playing. If you want an example of how to move cards around the base in groups, read on.

Look at the diagram above. Let's say that you want to move the 5♦ from Column 2 onto the 6♠ on the top of Column 6. This is how you'd do it. Move the 5♦ along with all of the cards on top of it in one big group, keeping them in the same order. When you've made the move, 3♥ will be the new top card of Column 2, and Column 6 will have the following cards in it: 6♣-9♥-4♣-10♠-6♠-5♦-Q♣-K♥-Q♠.

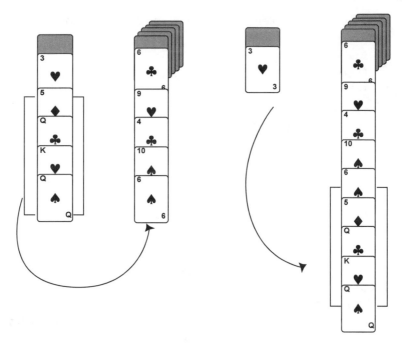

Redeals

You're not allowed any redeals.

Advice

☞ First, aim to uncover face-down cards. It's important to know where all the cards are, and you can't know that until you see their faces.

☞ Don't build on the foundation unless you have to. Good reasons for building on the foundation include uncovering a face -down card and helping to move cards around the base.

36. VICTORIA BALDWIN

In most games you get a break from thinking about strategy when you're collecting up the cards for a redeal. But not here. In *Victoria Baldwin*, the order in which you collect up the cards for the redeal is all part of the game's strategy. There are four piles, and you may collect them in any order you choose.

That's quite unusual for a solitaire game.

There is no base in this game; you deal cards from the pack into four wastepiles. The way you build these wastepiles is the key strategic element. You should pay careful attention to which cards you put in which pile. Later in the game you'll want to unpack the piles and be able to move all of the cards to the foundation.

Game type: Building
Aim: Build all of the cards onto the foundation
One game takes about: 10 minutes
Expect to win this game: Sometimes
Packs of cards: One

Set Up

Take the four aces out of the pack and lay them in a row. They form the foundation.

How To Win

To win, you must build the aces up in suit to kings.

How To Play

Deal the cards from the stock, four at a time. Put each card onto any of the four wastepiles. Any card can go on any pile, and you can put as many cards as you like in each. You can put all four cards into one pile, if that's what you want to do.

After you've dealt your four cards and put them into wastepiles, stop and move any top cards you can from the base to the foundation. The top card of each pile is in play between deals but not while you are dealing. In other words, you must wait until you've dealt those four cards before you move anything to the foundation. You aren't allowed to deal cards straight to the foundation—all cards must go to the wastepiles first.

In the wastepiles, you should overlap the cards as you deal them. This makes it easy to keep track of which cards are in which pile.

Redeals

When you've dealt all the cards and can make no more moves, you are allowed one redeal. Pick up the four base piles in any order you choose. Put one pile on top of another, but don't shuffle them. Keep the cards in order within their piles. Once you have gathered the cards together into one pile, it becomes your new stock. Deal the cards four at a time and play as normal.

Advice

☞ When deciding which pile to place your card in, follow this golden rule: Where possible, never put a higher card on a pile that already contains a lower card of the same suit.

☞ Also, think carefully about the order in which you pick up the four piles for the redeal. You should try to work it so that the highest cards are on the bottom of the new stock pile. That means you'll deal them last and they won't block the lower cards that you need early on.

37. POKER SOLITAIRE

Even if you've never played poker in your life, you'll be able to play this game. Everything you need to know is explained. The only thing that is the same as poker is the scoring system, so there's no bluffing, no raising, no chips and certainly no smoky rooms or green visors.

The key to *Poker Solitaire* is arranging your cards in the best possible way. You score points for certain combinations of cards. Unusually for solitaire, when you deal, you get to choose exactly where to put each card. You should place them where they will form high-scoring poker hands. The more points you win, the better.

You'll also notice below that the *Game type* is quite rare—it's a puzzle game. This is one of the few games that doesn't fit into the Fun or Strategy categories.

Game type: Puzzle
Aim: Arrange the cards to score the maximum number of points
One game takes about: 5 Minutes
Expect to win this game: Sometimes
Packs of cards: One

How To Play

Deal twenty-five cards, one at a time. Place each card into any unfilled position on a five-by-five grid. Each row and each column on the grid represents a poker hand of five cards.

A poker hand is just a group of five cards. Some combinations of cards are worth points. But more on that later.

In total, there are ten hands: five rows and five columns. The aim is to get the highest possible score from those ten hands. Once you place a card, you may not move it.

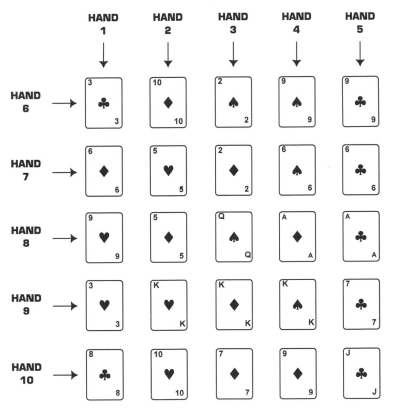

The following *How To Score* table gives you a list of what the different poker hands are and how many points you win for each of them. You should aim to score as many points as possible.

You'll notice that each card counts in two hands—one row and one column. For example, 5♦ is part of Hand 2 and also part of Hand 8.

There are two different ways to keep score, English and American. We'll explain below how these two systems work.

First, we'll quickly look at a couple of examples of how the cards form different hands. In our diagram, Hand 5 (9♣, 6♣, A♣, 7♣, 2♣) would be a **flush**, while Hand 9 (3♥,K♥,K♦,K♠,7♣) would be a **three of kind**. Those are examples. We did say it would be a quick look.

Here is the table to tell you which hands are worth points:

How To Score:

Name	Description	English Scoring	American Scoring
One Pair	One pair of the same rank + three odd cards 7♣ 7♥ 2♦ A♥ 9♠	1	2
Two Pairs	Two pairs of the same rank + one odd card 6♥ 6♦ J♣ J♥ 8♦	3	5
Three of a Kind	Three cards of the same rank + two odd two cards A♣ A♥ A♦ 9♥ J♦	6	10
Straight	Five cards in sequence, regardless of suit 8♦ 9♠ 10♠ J♥ Q♣	12	15
Flush	Five cards of the same suit, not in sequence 6♠ Q♠ 2♠ 4♠ 9♠	5	20
Full House	Three cards of the same rank + a pair of cards of another rank Q♠ Q♦ Q♥ 5♣ 5♥	10	25
Four of a Kind	Four cards of the same rank + any other card 2♦ 2♣ 2♥ 2♠ K♣	16	50
Straight Flush	Five cards in sequence, all of the same suit 4♣ 5♣ 6♣ 7♣ 8♣	30	75
Royal Flush	10-J-Q-K-A of the same suit 10♦ J♦ Q♦ K♦ A♦	30	100

As with regular poker, aces in any one hand can be high, ranking above kings, or low, ranking below 2s. You can't "turn the corner," however, so you are not allowed to have a sequence that goes from king to ace to 2. So, Q-K-A-2-3, for example, does not count as a **straight**.

Don't worry about the order of the cards within any one hand. If you've got a pair of 9s, they don't have to be right next to each other—so long as they are in the same hand, they count as a pair. Look at Hand 4 for an example of this.

Similarly, if you've got a straight the cards don't have to be in order. As long as they are all there, it counts as a straight. For an example of this, look at Hand 10. It contains an 8, 10, 7, 9, J. These form a straight even though they are not in order. All that matters is that all of the cards are in the same hand

How To Win

Score at least 70 English points or 200 American points.

Redeals

You're not allowed any redeals.

Advice

☞ Here is a word about the two different points systems. Once you know how each of them works, you'll be able to decide which one you want to use.

☞ English points reflect the difficulty of getting particular hands in *Poker Solitaire*. American points, on the other hand, reflect the difficulty of getting particular hands in regular poker.

38. SWITCH-A-ROO POKER SOLITAIRE

This game takes longer than *Solitaire Poker* and has more room for more strategy.

Game type: Puzzle
Aim: Arrange the cards to score the maximum number of points
One game takes about: 5 Minutes
Expect to win this game: Sometimes
Packs of cards: One

Play is the same as *Solitaire Poker*, except you are allowed to move the cards around after you've put them down. In fact, you can keep moving and swapping the cards around as much as you like until you put down the twenty-fifth card. Then you must stop switching and add up your points.

How To Win

Score at least 120 English points or 310 American points.

CHAPTER III
TRAVEL SOLITAIRE

In this chapter, you'll find all the solitaire games that are perfect for playing while you're traveling. They're also good for playing if you just don't have much room. And also, they're enjoyable games in themselves. So you don't need to be in cramped conditions to get out your cards and have a game or two.

Many of these travel games are based on other games that take up quite a lot of room. When this is the case, we have included the larger game ahead of the travel game. So don't be surprised when you see games in this chapter that aren't portable. They are there to explain how the portable games work. The portable games are marked with a "✈."

39. CANFIELD ✈

This is one of the most popular solitaire games around, and it certainly has one of the most interesting histories. It's named after Mr. Canfield who owned a casino in Saratoga Springs, New York, during the 1890s.

At the casino, gamblers could play *Canfield* for money. Mr. C. would "sell" a pack of cards for $50. The gambler would then play a game of *Canfield* solitaire, and the casino would pay $5 for every card in the foundation at the end of the game.

Although gamblers would usually make a loss—getting on average only five or six cards on the foundation—the game was very popular. Partly due to this popularity, Mr. Canfield became a wealthy man.

He always said, however, that *Canfield* wasn't as profitable as other casino games because you have to employ an attendant to watch each player. In roulette or blackjack, one croupier can tend to several gamblers.

Canfield is a classic building game. You deal cards from the stock into the wastepile, build on the base, and aim to get all the cards to the foundation. Oh, and if anybody asks you to put money on the game, run the other way.

Game type: Strategy
Aim: Build all of the cards onto the foundation
One game takes about: 6 minutes
Expect to win this game: Rarely
Packs of cards: One

Set Up

First, deal a pile of thirteen cards face down, then square the pile and turn it face up. This is the reserve. You deal it in this way so you can't see which cards are in the pile. From now on, all of the cards you deal in the game will be face up.

Now, to the left of the reserve pile deal one more card, face up. This is the first card of your foundation row.

Under that card deal a row of four cards, the base.

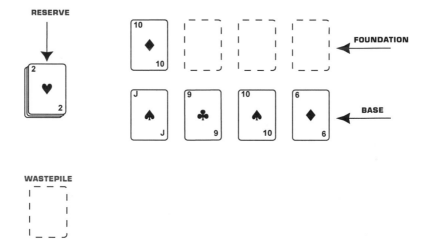

How To Play

Look at the first card on your foundation row. More specifically, look at the rank of that first card. In our example, the card is 10♦, so the rank is 10. That means you'd put 10♥, 10♣, and 10♠, if they become available, into those three foundation spaces.

Whatever the rank of that first card, you must fill the other three spaces with the same-ranked card from the other suits.

As soon as a foundation card is in place, you can start building on it. On the foundation, build up in suit and when you get to a king you carry on going up to ace then 2-3-4-5, and so on.

The top card of each pile in the base is always available for play. So is the top card of the reserve pile.

You may build available cards onto the foundation or on the top card of any base pile. When building on the base, you should build down in alternating colors.

Each time you get a gap in the base, you must fill it straight away with the top card from the reserve. If you run out of cards in the reserve pile, use the top card of the wastepile.

When you've used all of the cards in the reserve, you no longer have to fill gaps straight away—you can keep them open if you want to.

There is just one more rule that you have to follow when you're building. If you've built cards in sequence on the base, and you want to move them elsewhere on the base, you have to move those cards all together as one pile. You can't move just the top card. Remember, this rule only counts when you're moving cards around the base. So if you're transferring cards onto the foundation, you can only move the top card of a pile by itself.

Deal the stock into the wastepile in groups of three face up cards.

The rule for the wastepile throughout this game is this: only the top card is in play. If you use that top card, then the one underneath it becomes the new top card, and so on.

Keep playing in this way, dealing three cards from stock, pausing, playing what you can.

When you have dealt all of the cards, pick up the wastepile—be careful to keep the cards in order—and deal it out again in sets of three cards. You can keep redealing as many times as you want.

How To Win

To win, you must build up all of the cards onto the four foundation piles. It's very difficult to get more than six cards onto the foundation row, as Mr. Canfield well knew.

Redeals
You're not allowed any redeals in this game.

Advice
☞ Don't create a gap in the base until there is a useful card on top of the reserve to fill the gap. Once the reserve has run out, wait for a useful card on top of the wastepile. A useful card will probably be one that you'll soon be able to build on the foundation.

40. RAINBOW CANFIELD ✈
There is no getting around the fact that *Canfield* is a hard game to win. There are, however, quite a few variations on the original that are slightly easier or just put a different spin on things. Here, we've included the best variations, the first of which is *Rainbow Canfield*.

Game type: Strategy
Aim: Build all of the cards onto the foundation
One game takes about: 6 minutes
Expect to win this game: Rarely
Packs of cards: One

The set up, play and aim of the game are all the same as *Canfield*, but instead of dealing the cards into the wastepile in sets of three, deal them one at a time. You are allowed two redeals.

41. SELECTIVE CANFIELD ✈
This Selective Canfield allows you to choose which rank of card goes onto the foundation first. It gives you a slight advantage.

Game type: Strategy
Aim: Build all of the cards onto the foundation
One game takes about: 6 minutes
Expect to win this game: Rarely
Packs of cards: One

This is the same as *Canfield* apart from one small detail in the set up of the game. After you deal the thirteen-card reserve, deal a row of five face-up cards. Choose one of those five to be the first card of the foundation. The other four cards form the base, and you continue playing as you would a game of regular *Canfield*.

42. STOREHOUSE CANFIELD ✈

This is the *Canfield* variation that gives you the best chance of winning. Even if you don't win, the game will usually last longer, giving more time for cunning strategies.

Game type: Strategy
Aim: Build all of the cards onto the foundation
One game takes about: 8 minutes
Expect to win this game: Sometimes
Packs of cards: One

Play as you would a game of regular *Canfield* apart from one detail in the set up and two during play.
  1. Set up: Remove all four of the 2s from the pack and put them in the foundation row. Then deal the thirteen cards into the reserve and deal a row of four cards for the base.
  2. Play: While you are playing, deal cards one at a time into the wastepile.
  3. Redeals: Allow yourself two redeals.

43. ON THE ROAD ✈

This is perhaps the ultimate solitaire game for traveling. You hold the cards in your hand, so the game takes very little space. It also means that the cards won't get messed up if your driver takes a bend too sharply or your pilot hits turbulence at 35,000 feet.

You may end up with a lot of cards to hold, but don't worry. You only need to be able to see the top four, the rest you can put down or bunch up at the bottom of the fan.

In this discarding game, you look for pairs. When you find

them you get rid of them. The aim is to get rid of all the cards. In solitaire, there is a time to cast away cards, and a time to gather cards together. This is definitely a time to cast them away.

Game type: Fun
Aim: Get rid of all the cards
One game takes about: 4 Minutes
Expect to win this game: Sometimes
Packs of cards: One

How To Win
To win, you have to discard all of the cards.

How To Play
First, you should pick up four cards from the top of the pack. Hold them in a fan in your hand.

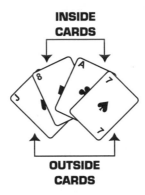

Look at the two outside cards: the cards at the right and left of the fan. If they are the same rank—two queens, for example, or two 7s—discard all four cards. If they are the same suit, discard just the two inside cards.

If you discarded a pair of cards, pick up two more from the pack. You'll be holding four cards again. Now, repeat the same process you went through with the original four cards. Keep repeating this process until you don't have any more pairs in the outside cards.

At this stage, you should start picking up new cards one at

a time from the pack. Add each one to the top of your fan. All the time, look only at the top four cards in your hand. After each new card, follow the same process of looking for pairs in the two outside cards.

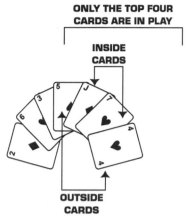

Each time you discard a pair of cards, look at the new top four cards and check whether you have a pair in the outside cards.

You are likely to build up quite a few cards in your hand, and there may not be room to fan all of them out. This doesn't matter, though, because you only ever need to be able to see the top four cards. If you find yourself with more cards than you can fan out in your hand, simply keep the top four cards fanned out and bunch up all of the other cards.

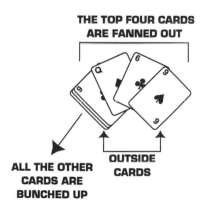

Redeals

You're not allowed any redeals.

Advice

☞ If you find that even when you bunch up your cards you still can't hold them in your hand, there is something else you can do. Simply put down the bottom cards instead of bunching them up. Once you've done this, you can just pick them up again if they become part of the top four.

44. DECADE

There are a few fun games that follow the same pattern as *Decade*. We've included them all in the same section here. They are easy to master and enjoyable to play. This is how they work:

One at a time, you deal all of the cards into one long row. After each card, you pause and look for a particular pattern—this might be matching pairs, or a group of cards that add up to a certain number. When you find cards that fit that pattern, you discard them. The aim of these games is to get rid of all your cards.

Sometimes the row of cards can become very long, and you might need to snake it around so that it fits on your table.

Most of these games have portable versions. We've included the portable versions after the originals. The portable versions all follow the same pattern as *Portable Solitaire*. So it's a good idea to learn that game first—it will give you a good idea of how the portable versions work.

With *Decade*, you're looking for groups of cards that add up to ten, twenty, or thirty. These groups must contain two or more cards, which must all be next to each other in the row.

Game type: Fun
Aim: Get rid of all the cards
One game takes about: 5 minutes
Expect to win this game: Rarely
Packs of cards: One

How To Play

Deal all of the cards, one at a time, into one long row. Pause after you deal each card and look out for groups of two or more cards next to each other that add up to ten, twenty or thirty. When you find such a group, discard all of the cards in it. In this game, jacks, queens, and kings are all worth ten each.

How To Win

Discard all of the cards.

Redeals

You're not allowed any redeals.

Advice

☞ Each time you discard, look back along the row to check whether you've created any new groups that add up to ten, twenty or thirty.

☞ It's very rare that you'll discard all of the cards. But if you finish up with eight cards or fewer, you've done well.

45. SEASON ✈

Here's the portable version of *Decade*.

Game type: Fun
Aim: Get rid of all the cards
One game takes about: 5 minutes
Expect to win this game: Rarely
Packs of cards: One

Play in exactly the same way as *Decade*, except instead of dealing the cards onto a table or surface, deal them into a fan in your hand. You may need to bunch up the cards at the bottom of the fan so that you have room to see the cards near the top.

46. ACCORDION

This game is long and thin to look at, but short and intense to play.

You deal the cards into one long row—and when we say long, we mean long. As you deal, you look out for matching pairs of cards. When you come across a pair, you pile up the cards. This means that you're unlikely to end up with all fifty-two cards next to each other in your row. During the game, you'll pile up the piles—if their top cards form pairs—and you'll aim to reduce your long row to as few piles as possible. If you end up with just one pile, you win.

Game Type: Fun
Aim: Get rid of all the cards
One Game Lasts: 4 minutes
Expect to Win: Rarely
Packs of cards: One

How To Play

All of the cards you deal in this game will be face up. Deal one card. Now deal another card and put it to the right of the first. Keep dealing cards, putting each to the right of the one before: the cards will form one long row.

After each card you deal, pause and compare it to the card immediately to its left and also to the card three to its left:

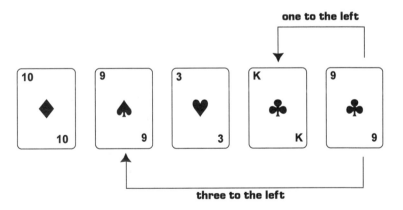

When a card is the same suit or rank as either of these cards, you can move the right hand card on top of the left hand card. So, in our example, you can move the 9♣ to one of two places:

a. 9♠, which is the same rank and three to the left

or

b. K♣, which is the same suit and next on the left

It's up to you which move you choose. It doesn't make a lot of difference now, but later on in the game it might. Most of the time, however, you won't have a choice because your card will only match one other, not two.

When you have two or more cards on top of each other, you create pile. With a pile you only look at the top card, and when you make a move you shift the whole pile.

In our example, let's say that you moved the 9♣ onto the 9♠. Now the 9♣ on the 9♠ is a pile. That means you only look at the 9♣, the top card. If you want to move that 9♣, you have to move the whole pile.

Each time you make a move, you should close up any gap left by the piles or cards that you've moved. Close up the gap by shifting all of the cards along to the left so that the cards form one continuous row.

How To Win

Get all of the cards into one pile.

Redeals

You're not allowed any redeals.

Advice

☞ It's rare that you will win this game. The cards don't usually let you. Even so, you should aim to get the minimum number of piles. Four piles is an excellent score.

47. SQUEEZEBOX ✈

If you like *Accordion*, you'll know that you can't play it on the back of a magazine on your lap while you're on a car or bus journey. The game is just too big.

That's why we developed *Squeezebox*. The game play is virtually the same as *Accordion*'s, but you deal the cards into a fan in your hand. So you can literally pick up the game and play it while you're on the move.

Don't worry about trying to fan out fifty-two cards in your hand—you only need to be able to see a few cards at any one time. So you can keep most of them bunched up. And don't worry about keeping track of piles, either. We've replaced them with a system of discarding cards instead of piling them up.

Game type: Fun
Aim: Get rid of all the cards
One game lasts about: 4 minutes
Expect to win this game: Rarely
Packs of cards: One

There are only two differences between this game and *Accordion*. One difference is where you put the cards, and the other is what to do when you get a matching pair.

1) Instead of dealing the cards onto a table, you deal the cards into a fan in your hand.

2) Each time you get a matching pair, move the card on the right so it is on top of the card on the left. The pair, remember, must either be one to the left or three to the left of another card. This part is the same as *Accordion*.

Now comes the difference.

After you've moved the right-hand card onto the left, you should discard the card that was on the left. In *Accordion* you pile the cards up when you move them, but in this game you just discard the cards that would be underneath the top card of each pile.

For example, say you had these cards in your hand:

Here, J♥ is the same suit as the card three to its left, 8♥. So you would move the J♥ to where the 8♥ is and then discard the 8♥. Your cards will end up looking like this:

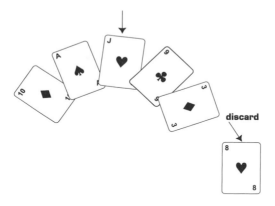

After you have shifted a card, check to see if you've created any more matching pairs. If you have, make your moves and discard any cards before you pick up your next card from the pack.

You may need to bunch up the cards on the bottom of your fan in order to see the top cards.

And at some points in the game, you may need to flick through the cards to see if you have created new matching pairs. Each time you discard a card, you'll need to look at the card that is one to the left and three to the left. Sometimes this process will require that you look through the cards that are bunched up at the bottom of your fan.

How To Win

You win the game when you've discarded all of the cards except for one.

Redeals

You're not allowed any redeals.

Advice

☞ As with *Accordion,* it's rare that you will win this game. If you have four cards in your hand at the end, you've done well.

48. DOUBLE JUMP

Set them up, line them up, and pile them up. That's what you do with the cards in this game. Oh, and when you get gaps, close them up.

To play, you lay out the cards in a row. If you find pairs that match in suit or rank, you put the right-hand one on top of the left hand one. The pairs have to be separated by two cards.

Game type: Fun
Aim: Get rid of all the cards
One game lasts: 6 minutes
Expect to win: Rarely
Packs of cards: One

How To Play

One by one, deal the entire pack of cards into one row, working from left to right. Keep an eye out for the following:

1. Two cards that are the same **rank** and are separated by two other cards

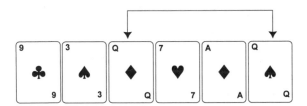

Or

2. Two cards that are the same **suit** and are separated by two other cards

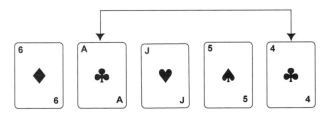

Whenever you come across either of these, you must perform the 'double jump'.

The Double Jump: There are two parts to the double jump.

Part 1: Place the left hand card on top of the right hand card. This is the first jump.

Part 2: Close up the gap where the left hand card was. You do this by shifting all of the cards to the right of that gap; shift them all to the left so that the gap is closed. This is the second jump.

In our examples, shown in the diagrams, your cards will look like this after the double jumps.

1a

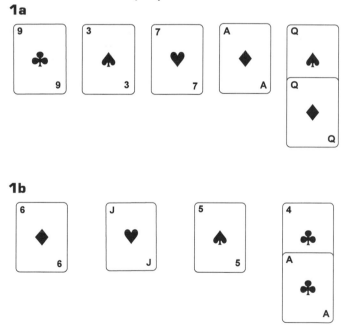

1b

After you've made your double jump, check to see whether any more double jumps are possible. If they are, make them. When you can't make any more double jumps, continue dealing the cards, one at a time, until you can jump again.

With each pile you make by performing step one of the double jump, you should only look at the top card. For example, with the cards in diagram (1a), there is a pile of queens at the far left. You'd only look at the top card, Q♦, and not at the card underneath, the Q♠. This rule applies no matter how many cards are in the pile. You should only ever look at the top card. Compare it to other cards to see if it matches rank or suit. If it does, treat the pile like a single card.

How To Win
End up with just three piles.

Redeals
You're not allowed any redeals.

Advice
☞ Each time you make a double jump, look back along the row and check whether you've created any new pairs. We're talking about pairs separated by two cards, of course, the ones that'll let you do another double jump. If you have created any, perform another double jump. And then check again.

49. PORTABLE DOUBLE JUMP ✈
Quite simply, this is a version of *Double Jump* that you can play while you're traveling, or if you don't have much space, or if, for some reason, you just prefer to hold the cards in your hand than lay them out on a table.

Game type: Fun
Aim: Get rid of all the cards
One game takes about: 8 minutes
Expect to win: Rarely
Packs of cards: One

This game is the same as *Double Jump*, except for two small things:
1. Instead of dealing the cards onto a table, deal them into a fan in your hand.

2. When you're making a double jump move the left hand card on top of the right hand card, and then discard the right hand card.

Apart from those two changes, play as you would with regular *Double Jump*.

You may need to bunch up the cards at the left hand side so you can fit them all in your hand.

How To Win
You win when you have discarded all of the cards except three.

Redeals
You're not allowed any redeals.

Advice
☞ If you find that even when you bunch up your cards you still can't hold them in your hand, there is something else you can do. Simply put down the bottom cards instead of bunching them up. Once you've done this, you can just pick them up again if they become part of the top four or if you need to look through them for pairs.

50. ACES UP
It moves quickly, it doesn't take up much room, there's a tiny bit of strategy involved, but essentially *Aces Up* is a fun game. You aim to discard cards. But instead of lining the cards up in a long row, like some of the other games in this chapter, you deal them onto just four piles. The way you discard cards is this: you look at the top card of each of those piles. If any of those cards are in the same suit, you get rid of the lowest cards. If you have 5♣ and Q♣, for example, it will be bye-bye 5.

Game type: Fun
Aim: Get rid of all the cards
One game lasts: 3 minutes
Expect to win: Sometimes
Packs of cards: One

Set Up

Deal a row of four cards.

How To Play

Look at those four cards. If there are any cards of the same suit, discard the lowest-ranking one. In this game, aces are the highest-ranking card—they are higher than kings.

Say, for example, that you have these four cards:

K♦, 9♣, 6♠, 5♣.

You have two clubs, 5♣ and 9♣. So you would discard 5♣ because it is the lower ranking one.

If you have three or four cards in the same suit, you discard all but the highest ranking one.

When you've made all the possible moves, fill in any gaps using the top card from any remaining pile. If there are fewer than four cards on the whole base, you should fill the gaps using cards from the stock.

After you've filled the gaps, check to see whether you can discard any more cards.

Continue to discard cards and fill gaps until you can't make any more moves. Then deal the stock in sets of four cards. Each time you deal, put one card on each of the four piles. Be sure to keep the piles spread out so you can see every card in every pile.

Keep going with this cycle of discarding the lowest-ranked cards, filling gaps, and adding a new layer of four cards. You should keep doing this until you have no more cards in the stock.

How To Win

The aces are the highest cards, so you will never discard them. But if you discard all of the cards apart from the four aces, you win the game.

Redeals

You're not allowed any redeals.

Advice

☞ The key to this game is choosing the right card to a fill

a gap. Look carefully to see which of the top cards you should place in a gap; you should try to uncover high cards. Also, where possible you should generally try to move aces into the gaps.

51. ROYAL FLUSH ✈

If you play poker, you'll know that the best hand you can get is a royal flush—10, jack, queen, king, ace all of the same suit. If you don't play poker, don't worry. You've already learnt the only thing you need to know: how to make a royal flush.

Unlike most discarding games, in which you have to get rid of all your cards, here you have to get rid of all your cards except five—those of a royal flush.

This is a great game. It's quick to learn, fast moving, and quick to play.

Game type: Fun
Aim: Get rid of all the cards
One game takes about: 3 minutes
Expect to win this game: Often
Packs of cards: One

Set Up

Deal all the cards face down into five piles. The first two piles should have eleven cards in, and the others should have ten.

How To Win

You get rid of cards throughout the game. We'll explain how in a minute. All you need to remember at this point is that to win you must end up with just five cards. Those five cards must be a 10, J, Q, K, A of the same suit. These are the cards that make up a royal flush, hence the name of the game. The cards don't have to be in the correct order. As long as you finish with these five cards in the same suit, you've won. Each time you play, you will select a suit at random for your royal flush.

How To Play

First, pick up the pile on the far left and turn it face up.

If you see a royal flush card—that's a 10, J, Q, K or A—on the top, the suit of this card decides the suit of the royal flush in this game. So if you had a J♣, for example, your royal flush will be in clubs.

There's a good chance this top card won't be a royal flush card. If it isn't, discard the cards in that pile one by one, starting with the top card and working your way down. Keep going until you come across a royal flush card.

If there isn't a single royal flush card in the first pile, follow the same process with the second pile, then third, and so on, until you find one. You are almost certain to find one in the first two piles.

When you find your first royal flush card, leave it on the top of its pile and don't discard any more of that pile's cards. The suit of that first royal flush card decides the suit of the royal flush for the whole game.

Now you've got that first card and you know what the suit of your royal flush will be. Next, you should go through each of the remaining piles, moving from left to right. Turn each pile face up and, if you need to, discard the cards one by one until you come across one of the other cards from the royal flush that you're looking for.

If the first royal flush card was J♣, as it is in our example, we'd be looking for 10♣, Q♣, K♣, and A♣.

As before, when you find one of the cards you're looking for, leave it on the top of its pile and move on to the next pile. If you go through a whole pile and there are no cards you want, just move on to the next pile and keep looking.

When you have been through all of the piles, each remaining one will have a card from your royal flush on top.

Redeals

At this stage in the game, you have to redeal. To do this, you should stack up the remaining piles in order. Put the pile at the far right on top of its left-hand neighbor. Then put that new pile onto its own left-hand neighbor, repeat this process for each pile until you are left with just one pile. Don't collect up the cards you discarded earlier on.

Redeal your newly formed pile, dealing the cards face down as you did with the original set up. This time, however, deal them into just four piles instead of five. And distribute the cards evenly among the four piles.

Repeat the process of turning up the piles, looking for royal flush cards, discarding other cards and redealing. The next time you redeal, put the cards into three piles. And the next time, deal into just two.

When you come to the next and final redeal, deal the cards into just one pile.

Now when you get to this final deal, you hope to be left with just the cards in your royal flush—a 10, J, Q, K, A. They should all be in the suit of that first royal flush card you turned up. In our example, it was J♣. These cards don't have to be in the correct order. As long as you have these five cards and no others, you've won.

Advice

☞ With many solitaire games, you get an idea whether you're going to win a while before the end. But with *Royal Flush* it's nearly always down to the wire. Often you can't tell whether you'll win until the last round.

☞ You can try playing this game aiming to create other hands, not just royal flushes. (For a list of other poker hands, look at the table on page 78.) You could try making a full house, a straight, a straight flush.

☞ There are two ways to make these changes—one easy, one hard.

☞ For the easy version, simply decide which hand you're going for. And as cards come up, leave them on the top of their piles and move on to the next pile. You have to remember which cards you were including, and keep them the same throughout the game.

☞ For the hard version, you must specify exactly which cards you are looking for. Let's say you decide to go for a full house. You'd have to decide exactly which cards you'll look for —three queens and two 10s, for example.

52. ROYAL MARRIAGE

You might like to think of this game as a royal court. Pairs of sweethearts come along, but one or both of the bride's parents will stand in the way of their marrying. You, however, get to play cupid and take the parents out of the equation, leaving the sweethearts free to tie the knot.

Of course, after they get married, some of them will become awkward parents themselves, and some of them will divorce and remarry. But everything is done with the intention of getting the king and queen together in the end to live happily ever after. Until the next game, that is.

How does all this translate into a solitaire game? Well, the sweethearts are pairs of cards that have the same suit or rank and are separated by one or two other cards, the meddling parents. The king and the queen are the K♥ and Q♥, which are at opposite ends of the pack of cards. In order to arrange their royal marriage, you have to eliminate all of the cards between them.

Game type: Fun
Aim: Get rid of all the cards
One game takes about: 2 minutes
You should win this game: Sometimes
Packs of cards: One

Set Up

First, you should take the Q♥ and K♥ out of the pack. Put the Q♥ on the far left of the table and the K♥ on the very bottom of the pack. The K♥ will be the last card you deal.

How To Win

As you might have guessed from this game's name—or from reading its introduction—to win you must make the king and queen of hearts "marry" each other. You arrange their marriage by getting rid of all the cards that come between them.

How To Play

Deal all the cards, one at a time. Put the first card to the right of the Q♥, and keep putting each card to the right of the one before. You will form a row going from right to left.

After each card you deal, pause and look to see whether the row contains any pairs of the same rank—9s, jacks, etc.—or of the same suit. These pairs must have either one or two cards between them. Look at this diagram:

The Q♥ and Q♠ are the same rank and they have one card separating them, 5♠. So you would discard that card. Also, the 4♦ and the 9♦ are the same suit and have two cards separating them, so you would discard both of the separating cards, 2♣ and 6♠.

After you've discarded those in-between cards, close up the gaps they leave behind. Close up the gaps by shifting all of the cards to the right of that gap. Shift them all to the left, so that all of the cards make a continuous row.

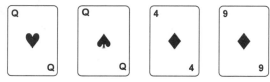

Now look to see if the shake up has created any more of these pairs.

In our example, there aren't any new pairs. So you would continue dealing the cards, one by one, until another pair shows up.

Redeals

You're not allowed any redeals.

Advice

☞ Each time you discard, look back along the row and check whether you've created any new pairs. If you have, discard and then check again.

53. VEGAS WEDDING

Royal Marriage has gone to Vegas. The game is the same, but you can play it while you're traveling. How is this possible? you ask. Well, you hold the cards in your hand; this makes it easy to play while you're on the move or if you have limited space.

Game type: Fun
Aim: Get rid of all the cards
One game takes about: 2 minutes
You should win this game: Sometimes
Packs of cards: One

In this version, the rules stay exactly the same. The only difference is that instead of dealing the cards onto a table or floor, you deal the cards into a fan in your hand.

So to start the game put the Q♥ as the first card in your fan and put the K♥ on the bottom of the pack. Now deal the cards one at a time on top of the Q♥, making them into a fan. Continue play as you would in a normal game of *Royal Marriage*.

If you end up with a large number of cards in your fan, you may need to bunch up the cards on the left hand side. Then, if you need to look through those bottom cards for any reason, you can always flick through them or spread them out for a short while.

54. PERPETUAL MOTION ✈

This is undoubtedly one of the best fun solitaire games around. It's ideal for traveling because it doesn't take up much space, and each game lasts about an hour so it's good for whiling away the time during long journeys.

You aim to get rid of all your cards, but you can only discard cards when you have four of the same rank. This is tricky because there are only four spaces on the base. But with unlimited redeals and a handy little built-in system that groups like cards together, you are able win more often than you might expect.

Game type: Fun, lots of fun
Aim: Get rid of all the cards
One game takes about: 1 hour
Expect to win this game: Sometimes
Packs of cards: One

How To Win

To win, you must discard all of the cards. You discard them in sets of four cards that are of the same rank.

How To Play

First, you should deal a row of four cards. Check to see whether it contains any cards of the same rank. Remember, rank means the number or name of the card—5, 9, or king, for example.

If all four cards are the same rank, discard all of them. And if there are two or three cards of the same rank—two 9s, for example, or three jacks—move all of those cards onto the one furthest to the left.

Here's an example of that. Let's say you dealt these cards:

5♠ 5♦ Q♠ 5♣

There are three cards of the same rank—5s. So you would move the 5♦ and the 5♣ on top of the 5♠, which is the 5 furthest to the left.

You should deal out the entire pack in sets of four cards, placing one on each of the four piles.

After you deal each set of four cards, check to see if you have any cards of the same rank. If you do, move them accordingly.

As long as you are not in the process of dealing, the top card of each pile is available for play. So after you've made your moves, check to see if you've uncovered any more cards of the same rank and if you have, move them too.

Remember, each time you have four cards of the same rank showing, you should discard all of them.

Redeals

When you've dealt all the cards in the pack, collect up the four piles in the following way. Put Pile 4 on top of Pile 3. Then put that new pile on top of Pile 2. And then put *that* new pile on top of Pile 1. You'll end up with just one pile. This forms the stock.

Be careful to keep the piles in this order.

Now deal the cards from the stock in sets of four and play as you did before. You can keep redealing in this way as many times as you like.

Advice

☞ This is a fast game, if you want it to be, and you can add an extra element of fun if you make it even faster. Try timing yourself while you play. As well as seeing how many cards you get left over, record how long it takes you to get to the end of the game.

55. HIT OR MISS ✈

You're trying to get rid of all your cards. And you're trying to do it in the following way. Deal the cards into a single pile. But while you deal, you say the names of the cards in order. If the card you deal is the same as the card you say, you get to discard it. Of course, you don't have to speak out loud. If you prefer, you can say the names of the cards in your head. And you'll probably want to use the silent option if you're playing this game while you're traveling.

It's a simple concept, but it takes real concentration to play. You might find it almost like meditating. Some people think that repeating the numbers and names is like saying a mantra.

Game type: Fun
Aim: Get rid of all the cards
One game takes about: 15 minutes
Expect to win this game: Rarely
Packs of cards: One

How To Play

Deal the cards one at a time onto a single pile. As you deal the first card, say "ace"; as you deal the second card, say "two"; with third card say "three"; the fourth card "four"; and so on. After "ten" comes "jack," then "queen," and then "king." And after you've said king, start at ace again. You can say these cards' names either out loud or in your head.

Each time the card you deal matches the card you say, that is a "hit." And each time you get a hit, you discard that card. Because the aim is to discard all your cards, hits are good things.

Redeals

When you've dealt all the cards, pick up the pile. Keep the cards in order, turn the pile over, and deal it out again saying the names of the cards while you do so.

Each time you pick up the pile, remember the last card you said and continue from the next card. So if the last card you said was "eight," you would say "nine" when you deal the first card of your redeal.

You can redeal as many times as you like. But if you go through the pack twice in a row without a single hit, the game is over.

How To Win

If you discard all of the cards, you win the game.

Advice

☞ You should play to win, naturally. But you should also record your best scores. It's very difficult to win outright, but you can always improve.

56. SUPER HIT OR MISS ✈

If you've got a long journey ahead and you want something to keep you occupied, this is the game for you. It can last for quite a while.

Game type: Fun
Aim: Get rid of all the cards
One game takes about: 25 minutes
Expect to win this game: Usually (if you have enough time)
Packs of cards: One

Play as you would a game of regular *Hit or Miss*, but you are allowed unlimited redeals no matter what. So even if you go through the pack twice without a hit, you are allowed to continue redealing.

You're likely to win the game eventually, unless, that is, you get no hits when you have 13, 26, 39 or 52 cards in your pile.

57. ULTIMATE HIT OR MISS ✈

This is the ultimate long-journey game. If you want to fill a long space of time playing solitaire, look no further.

Game type: Fun
Aim: Get rid of all the cards
One game takes about: 60 minutes
Expect to win this game: Usually (if you have enough time)
Packs of cards: Two

Play in exactly the same way as *Super Hit or Miss*, except use two packs of cards shuffled together.

CHAPTER IV
FUN GAMES

58. CLOCK

It's time for some pure fun. In this game there's no strategy to think about, no planning to do, and no decisions to make. You just deal out those cards, check your free will at the door, and enter Club Predestination, a very relaxing place. But even though you don't have to work out a strategy, *Clock* is still engaging and enjoyable to play.

The aim of this game is unique. You deal out the cards face down, follow one simple rule and turn up cards one by one. The kings are the rulers of this game, and you must keep track of how many you turn up. If you have turned all of the other cards face up before you turn up the fourth king, you win.

Game type: Fun
Aim: Turn all the cards face up before the game ends
One game takes about: 5 minutes
Expect to win this game: Rarely
Packs of cards: One

Set Up

Deal thirteen piles. Each should have four cards in it. Lay out the piles in a circle like a clock face. Put one pile in the middle, and put the other twelve in a circle around it, one where each of the twelve numbers on a clock would be.

You'll notice on the diagram that the piles are all labeled with the names of cards. These labels are important for the game. We'll explain them a bit later.

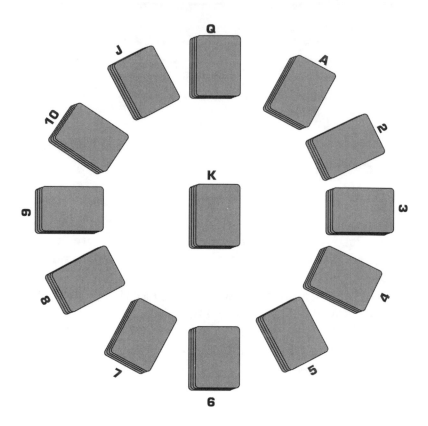

How To Play

Pick up the card on the top of the middle pile, that's the pile labeled "K" on the diagram. Put that card face up on the bottom of the pile of its own number. Then pick up the top card from *that* pile and put it face up on the bottom of the pile of its own number. Keep repeating this process.

Here's an example to show you how it works. Let's say the card you pick up from the center pile is a 10. You'd put that 10 face up at the bottom of the pile labeled "10" on the diagram.

Now you pick up the top card from the "10" pile and put it face up at the bottom of the pile of its own number. If you picked up an ace, for example, you'd put it underneath the "A" pile.

Carry on doing this until you have turned up all four kings and placed them face up in the "K" pile.

Throughout the game, you may only turn over face-down cards. Sometimes you'll put a card to the bottom of a pile and find that there are no more face-down cards on top of it, all of its cards will be face up. If this happens, just go clockwise to the next pile that does have face-down cards on it. Then pick up the top card from that pile and keep on playing.

It's easy to remember which rank goes where in this game because, for the most part, the piles correspond to the numbers on a clock face.

How To Win

You win the game if when you pick up the fourth king there are no more face down cards on any pile. If there is even one face down card when you pick up that fourth and final king, you don't win.

Redeals

There are no redeals in this game.

Advice

☞ Some players find they accidentally keep playing after they've turned up the fourth king. If this happens to you, try fanning the kings out so that it's obvious when all four are face up.

59. WATCH

This is similar to *Clock*, but slightly less severe. You get a second chance to win.

Game type: Fun
Aim: Turn all the cards face up before the game ends
One game takes about: 5 minutes
Expect to win this game: Rarely
Packs of cards: One

Play in exactly the same way as *Clock*, except for one difference. If you turn up the fourth king before the end of the game, you can swap it with any other face down card. There is not a third chance, though. So if you turn up that fourth king again—you loose the game.

60. PYRAMID

The cards in this game are set up in the shape of a pyramid. You have to match up and discard pairs that add up to thirteen. When you get stuck, you can deal cards from the stock to help you make pairs. Get rid of all your cards and you win the game.

Game type: Fun
Aim: Get rid of all the cards
One game takes about: 5 minutes
Expect to win this game: Sometimes
Packs of cards: One
Category: Discarding

Set up

Deal twenty-eight cards into a pyramid formation. You should start by dealing a single card. Then overlap it with a row of two cards. And then overlap that with a row of three. Continue adding rows, with one extra card in each, until you have seven rows. The seventh row will contain seven cards.

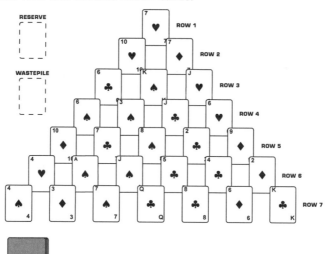

How To Win

To win, you must discard all fifty-two cards into the wastepile. You discard them in pairs that add up to thirteen.

In this game, jacks =11, queens = 12, kings = 13, and aces = 1.

How To Play

A card is in play if no other card overlaps it. So at the very start of the game, the only cards in play are those in Row 7.

You have to remove pairs of cards that add up to thirteen.

Here is a quick guide to all of the pairs that add up to thirteen:

2 and jack	3 and 10	4 and 9
5 and 8	6 and 7	ace and queen

Kings are also worth thirteen, so you may remove them on their own. Don't put discarded cards in the wastepile. Put them somewhere else. Once a card is discarded it is out of the game completely, whereas cards in the wastepile are still in play.

Let's look at an example. Say you have the cards in our diagram, you would start by removing K♣, because kings are worth 13. Then you would remove 7♠ and 6♦, because 7 and 6 equal 13.

After you'd removed K♣ and 6♦, there would be no cards overlapping 2♦, so now 2♦ would now be available for play. This means you could remove the 2♦ and the Q♣.

Deal the stock, one card at a time. If it forms a pair with an available card—you may discard both cards in the pair. If it is a king, you can discard it also. Put unplayable cards from the stock into the wastepile. The top card of the wastepile is always in play. That means you can discard it if it's a king or if it forms a pair that adds up to thirteen with one of the cards in play in the pyramid or a card you deal from the stock.

So let's go back to our example. After you remove the 2♦ and Q♣, there are no more pairs of thirteen and no more kings. This means you have to start dealing the pack into the wastepile. The first card you deal is Q♥. There are no aces available, so deal a second card onto the reserve. This second card is 10♣—so you would remove that along with the 3♦ because 10+3 = 13.

Once you remove the 10♣, the Q♥ is back on the top of the reserve pile and so it is in play. And now that you have removed the 3♦, the A♣ isn't overlapped by any other cards, so that too is in play. Queen plus ace equals thirteen, so you can remove both of them.

Redeals

There are no redeals in this game.

Advice

☞ After you've set up the cards and before you do anything else, deal one card from the stock into the wastepile. You'll have to do this eventually, and doing it right away gives you an extra option.

☞ You should never have an empty wastepile. Always keep a minimum of one card in it. This gives you the maximum number of options to make pairs. The only times when you should have an empty wastepile is when you have discarded all of the cards and won the game.

61. BARONESS

Give it away, now. That is your motto while playing *Baroness*. You must try to get rid of all the cards. Doing this, however, is harder that it looks because you can only discard them in pairs that add up to thirteen.

Game type: Fun
Aim: Get rid of all the cards
One game lasts: 4 minutes
Expect to win: Sometimes
Packs of cards: One

Set Up

Deal a row of five cards.

How To Play

Thirteen is the magic number in this game. Look at the top card of each of those five piles. Whenever you get a king discard it—kings are worth thirteen, remember. And if any two cards add up to thirteen, discard both of them.

In this game the picture cards and aces have the following values:

Jack = 11   Queen = 12   King = 13   Ace = 1

Here is a quick guide to all of the pairs that add up to thirteen:

2 and jack	3 and 10	4 and 9
5 and 8	6 and 7	ace and queen

Fill each gap with the top card from any other pile. If there aren't enough cards in the other piles to do this, use a card from the stock.

When you have filled all the gaps and there are no more kings and no more pairs that add up to thirteen, deal another layer of five cards, one on each pile. Keep repeating the process until there are no more cards in the stock.

How To Win

If you discard all of the cards, you win.

Redeals

There are no redeals in this game.

Advice

☞ Keep the cards in the wastepiles spread out. This lets you keep track of where cards are. And you need to know that to make the best possible choices when deciding which pairs to move.

☞ Sometimes you'll have a choice of pairs. One card will add up to thirteen with two possible others. When faced with this type of decision, you should pick the pair that will lead you to the most other pairs.

62. EVEREST

Game type: Fun
Aim: Get rid of all the cards
One game lasts: 4 minutes
Expect to win: Sometimes
Packs of cards: One

Play as you would a normal game of *Baroness*, except for one difference. Have two rows of five instead of just one row. When you set up, deal ten cards; and when you deal from the stock each time, deal ten cards—one onto each pile.

63. FOURTEEN PUZZLE

Less is definitely more in this game, which is all about getting rid of cards. The fewer cards you have at the end, the better. And if you end up with no cards at all, you win. As the name of this game suggests, fourteen is the magic number here. You're only allowed to discard cards in pairs that add up to fourteen.

Game type: Fun
Aim: Get rid of all the cards
One game takes about: 5 Minutes
Expect to win this game: Often
Packs of cards: One

Set Up

Deal all of the cards face up in twelve overlapping columns. Put five cards in the first four columns and four cards in all of the rest.

How To Play

The top card of each column is available for play. Remove available cards in pairs that add up to fourteen. In this game, the picture cards are worth the following:

Jack = 11   Queen = 12   King = 13   Ace = 1

Here is a list of pairs that add up to fourteen:

ace and king	5 and 9
2 and queen	6 and 8
3 and jack	7 and 7
4 and 10	

How To Win

To win, you must remove all the cards.

Redeals

There are no redeals in this game.

Advice

☞ As with other games where you discard in pairs, sometimes you'll have a choice of pairs. One card will pair up with two possible others. When faced with this type of decision, you should pick the pair that will lead to the most other pairs.

64. NESTOR

This is Operation Get Rid of Pairs. Rule number one: If it's in a pair, discard it. You should remove cards in pairs of the same rank and aim to get rid of all the cards. Got that, soldier? Good. Now get down and start dealing.

Game type: Fun
Aim: Get rid of all the cards
One game takes about: 5 Minutes
Expect to win this game: Sometimes
Packs of cards: One

Set Up

Deal eight columns of six cards. Overlap the cards so that you can see them all. No column may contain two cards of the same rank. So if you deal a 7, for example, and there is already a 7 in the column you are dealing to, put the second 7 to the bottom of the pack and deal another card instead.

There will be four cards left over. These form the reserve. Place them face down below the base.

How To Play

You must remove available cards in pairs of the same rank, two 6s or two queens, for example. The top card of each column and each card in the reserve is available for play.

Each time you get totally stuck, turn over one card from the reserve. When a reserve card is face up, it is available for play. So you may use this card to form pairs as you would any other available card.

How To Win

If you discard all of the cards, you win.

Redeals

There are no redeals in this game.

Advice

☞ As with other games where you discard in pairs, sometimes you'll have a choice of pairs. One card will pair up with two possible others. When faced with this type of decision, you should pick the pair that will allow you to make the most other pairs later on.

65. GAPS

Gaps is a cross-breed. It has the appearance of a building game, but the heart of a fun one.

The game starts off with all the cards laid out in a grid with four gaps in it. You have to fill these gaps using cards from elsewhere on the layout. But when you move a card to fill a gap, that card leaves a new gap. Guess what. You have to fill that gap too. Every time you fill a gap, you create a new one.

There is a built-in system that means you'll tend to build the cards in sequence from left to right. There's also another system that means that gaps can become blocked—this stops the game from being too easy. Even if your gaps do become blocked, however, you're allowed three redeals.

Game type: Fun
Aim: Put all the cards in sequence on the base
One game takes about: 10 Minutes
Expect to win this game: Rarely
Packs of cards: One

Set up

Deal four rows, each with thirteen face up cards in it. When you've finished, discard the four aces. This will leave four gaps in your layout.

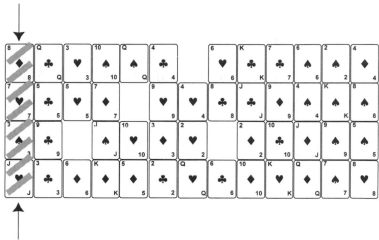

The 2 Zone: If you get a gap here, you must fill it with a 2.

How To Win

Get each of the four rows to contain twelve cards in suit going up in sequence from 2 on the far left hand side to king on the right.

How To Play

This game is all about filling gaps. Look at the card to the left of each gap. Whatever that card is, find the card that is one rank higher in the same suit and place that card in the gap. On our example, look at the gap on the second row. The card to the left of this gap is 7♦, so you'd put the 8♦ into the gap. Of course, when you move the 8♦ you create a new gap, which you must then fill.

When you get a gap in the left-most card of any of the four rows, fill it with the 2 of your choice. We have marked this area "The 2 Zone" on the diagram.

You may not fill a gap that has a king to the right of it.

Redeals

Eventually you will get to a stage where all of your gaps have kings to the right of them. That means you can't make any more moves.

When this happens, collect up all of the cards that are not in suit sequence starting with a 2 on the left-most card of their row. On the following diagram—you would collect all of the cards except the ones shaded in.

This shows a different game to the previous diagram. The game here has come to a halt because all of the gaps are blocked by kings.

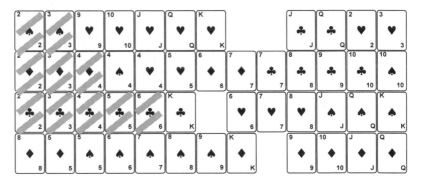

Do not collect in the aces which you discarded earlier.

Once you have collected all of the remaining cards, shuffle them thoroughly and redeal them in the following way. Deal from left to right, row by row. For each row, leave a one-card gap between the last card on the left and the first card you deal. This diagram shows how your layout should look when you've redealt.

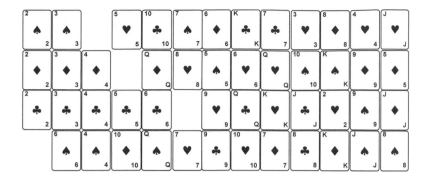

After you've redealt the cards, fill the gaps as you were doing before.

You may redeal three times in total.

Advice

☞ Sometimes you'll have two gaps to the left of a king. When this happens, both gaps are blocked. There's not much you can do about this, or about any other gap getting blocked. The outcome of the game is determined by the luck of the draw. *Gaps* shows that games without strategy can be plenty of fun and interesting to play again and again.

66. TRICKLE DOWN

Sometimes at weddings or special events, you'll find a pyramid of champagne glasses carefully piled on top of one another, all standing the right way up. Someone will pour champagne into the top glass. When that becomes full, the liquid overflows into the glasses in the next row. As the glasses in each row become full, the liquid runs down and fills up those on the next level down, eventually working its way to the bottom.

Building on the foundation in this game works on a similar principal. There are four foundation rows, one for each suit. You may only build a card onto a row if the same-ranked card is already in the row above.

For example, you can't put a king into a row unless there is already a king in the row above. On the top row, you can build anything, as long as it's the correct suit—this is like pouring the champagne into the top glass. In this way, the ranks trickle down the four foundation rows from top to bottom.

Game type: Fun
Aim: Build all of the cards onto the foundation
One game takes about: 15 minutes
Expect to win this game: Sometimes
Packs of cards: One

Set Up

Deal four piles, each containing three face-down cards. Next to the first pile, deal a single card face up.

When you deal those four piles, deal them face down, square them up, and finally turn them over. This means that all the cards will now be face up, but you'll be able to see the top one of each pile. Doing this means that you can't see what's in each pile, and that's important for the game to work.

How To Win

To win, you must build all of the cards onto the foundation. If you win, each of the four rows will end up containing all thirteen cards in its suit.

How To Play

We'll use the cards shown in the diagram to illustrate the rules. As usual, the top card of each reserve pile is available for play.

Let's say the first card in the foundation is a 4, the 4♦. So as the other 4s become available, we'll put them in the other three foundation spaces. Those spaces are marked with dotted lines on the diagram.

If you have the 4♣ on the reserve, you can put that into the second foundation row straight away.

The next 4 we come across will go in the third row, and the last one will go in the fourth row.

The rule for the foundation, then, is that the first card in the foundation decides the rank. As the other three cards of the same rank become available, you place them into the foundation.

On the top foundation row, you can build any card in the same suit as that first card, regardless of sequence.

When you build on the foundation, build sideways and overlap the cards so that you can see what each one is.

On the second, third and fourth rows, you build in suit regardless of sequence, but you can only build a card that is already in the row above.

Deal the cards from the stock three at a time onto the wastepile. The top card of this pile is available for play onto the foundation.

Redeals

When you've dealt the entire stock, pick up the wastepile and turn it over. It becomes the new stock. Now deal it out again in sets of three, making sure you keep the cards in order. You can redeal as many times as necessary—you will eventually get stuck or win the game.

Advice

☞ There is a way to add a touch of strategy to this purely fun game. Simply spread out the cards in the four reserve piles. This lets you know what each one contains. Once you know this, you can make informed decisions about the order in which you should add the last three suits to the foundation. If the reserve contains a high number of cards from a particular suit, then it's often a good plan to make that the second suit to go into the foundation. In other words, if the reserve is full of hearts, put hearts on the second foundation row. This won't always be possible, but it's something to aim for.

67. THE COOMBES

This is a slightly more strategic version of *Trickle Down*.

Game type: Fun
Aim: Build all of the cards onto the foundation
One game takes about: 15 minutes
Expect to win this game: Sometimes
Packs of cards: One

Play by exactly the same rules as *Trickle Down*, but with one difference. Spread out the cards in the reserve piles before you start play. This may show you that you should lay the first foundation cards in a particular order to avoid potential blocks in the reserve. *The Wiltons* allows you more room for strategy than its parent game, *Trickle Down*.

68. MONTE CARLO

Once again, it's better to discard than to receive. In this game you're aiming to get rid of all your cards. But this time you have to look for pairs—two 7s, two queens, in fact any pair of cards that are the same rank. If those two cards are next to each other, you are allowed to cast them both out. There is only one other thing to think about. If you get rid of all your cards and win the game, should that be called the full monte?

Game type: Fun
Aim: Get rid of all the cards
One game takes about: 8 Minutes
Expect to win this game: Sometimes
Packs of cards: One

Set Up

Deal five rows of five cards each. They should form a five-by-five grid.

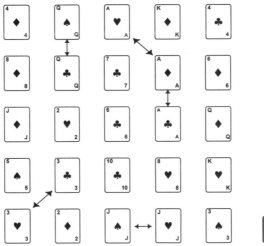

How To Win

If you discard all the cards, you win. You may only discard cards in pairs they are of the same rank and are next to each other in the grid.

How To Play

Remove pairs of cards that are the same rank and are next to each other. The pairs can be:

1. One above the other, like Q♠ and Q♣ in the diagram;
2. Side by side, like J♠ and J♥; or,
3. Touching diagonally, like 3♣ and 3♥.

Sometimes a card will be paired with two others of the same rank. If this happens you have to decide which pair you want to remove—you're only allowed to remove one. For an example of this, take a look at the A♦ on the diagram. It is paired with two cards of the same rank: A♥ and A♣. You may only remove one of the pairs—either A♦ and A♥, or A♦ and A♣. For the purpose of our example, we'll choose to remove A♦ and A♥.

The two cards in the pair must be right next to each other. If you remove a pair and you are left with two cards that are the same rank and are separated only by a gap, this does not count as a pair.

For example, let's say we removed 3♥ and 3♣. This would mean the 2♥ and 2♦ were one above the other, but separated by a gap where the 3♣ was. These two 2s are not a proper pair, so you can't remove them.

When you've removed all of the pairs, you must fill up the grid so that it contains five rows of five again. Do this by shifting the cards along to fill up the gaps; you must shift them in the following way.

1. Start by looking at your top row of cards. If you have any gaps there, shift the cards to the left to close up those gaps.
2. Then fill the gaps at the right hand side of the top row using the leftmost cards of the next row down.
3. When your top row is full again and contains five cards, you should repeat the whole process with the next row down,

then the next row. You should keep working your way down until you get to the bottom row.

We'll give an example of how this would work with the cards in our diagram, and then we'll tell you the final thing you need to know about filling gaps.

Let's say that in our example, shown in the diagram, we have two gaps in the top row. We created the gaps by removing the Q♠ and A♥. You would move K♦ along to where Q♠ was, and then you'd move 4♣ along to where the A♥ was.

Now you have two gaps at the far right of the top row. Fill these gaps using the leftmost cards from the row below. In our example, we'd move 8♦ to where K♦ was, and then A♣ to where 4♣ was.

Here is a handy little diagram that illustrates the rules of shifting and shows you the direction in which to shift the cards:

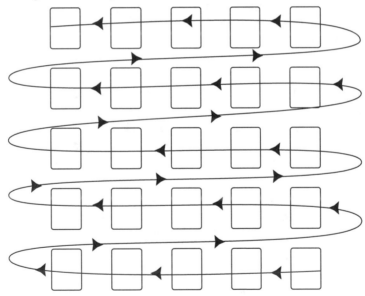

After you've closed up all of the gaps, you will have spaces in the bottom right hand corner. Fill these spaces from the stock so that, after all your shifting and filling, you're left with five rows of five. That's all you need to know about filling gaps.

Once all your gaps are filled, you should continue play by removing pairs of cards next to each other. Each time you get stuck, close up the gaps, fill the spaces, and then continue.

Redeals

There are no redeals in this game.

Advice

☞ Sometimes you'll have a choice of pairs. One card will pair up with two possible others. When faced with this type of decision, you should pick the pair that will allow you to make the most other pairs later on.

69. CAPTIVE QUEENS

It's the age of chivalry. Brave knights are making dragons an endangered species. The invention of the catapult has made castle insurance very expensive. And you, for the purpose of this game, are a villain who will capture four queens and build a prison to trap them in.

When building your prison, you make your foundation out of 5s and 6s. Then you build up walls on top of the 6s to stop the queens clambering over the prison walls. And to stop those crafty royals tunneling away to freedom, you also build underground walls down on the 5s.

If by the end of the game you have built all of the cards onto the foundation, your captives remain imprisoned and you can demand a queen's ransom for them. If, however, you didn't manage to build all the cards onto the foundation, the queens will make a great escape. If you want them back, you'll just have to start another game.

Game type: Fun
Aim: Build all of the cards onto the foundation
One game takes about: 5 Minutes
Expect to win this game: Often
Packs of cards: One

How To Win

To win, you must build all of the cards, except the queens, onto the foundation.

How To Play

Deal the cards one at a time from the stock, placing them on the wastepile. The top card of this wastepile is always available for play. After dealing each card, you should pause to see whether you can build it onto the foundation. When you come across a 5 or a 6, put it on the foundation. The foundation is circular, and any 5 or 6 can go in any position.

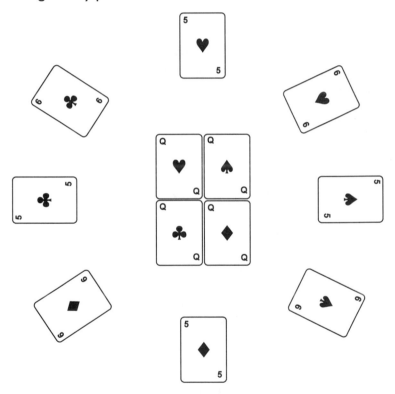

You can start building on a 5 or a 6 as soon as you put it in the foundation.

On the 5s, build down in suit to king: 5-4-3-A-K
And on the 6s build up in suit to jack: 6-7-8-9-10-J

When you come across a queen, put her in the middle of the circle and leave her there. She is your captive.

Redeals

When you've dealt all of the cards from the stock into the wastepile, you may turn over the wastepile to form a new stock. Redeal these cards and play as normal. This is a redeal; you are allowed two of them.

Advice

☞ You should build on the foundation at every opportunity.

☞ A different way to play this game is to allow yourself unlimited redeals and count how many it takes you to complete the game. You should be able to do it in three.

CHAPTER V
STRATEGY,
TWO PACKS

All of the games in this chapter require two packs of cards. It's best if you use two identical packs and shuffle them together. Then use this double-pack as you would a regular, 52-card one. Take out all the jokers before you start playing.

Remember that you now have eight aces, instead of four, and twenty-six cards, instead of thirteen, in each suit, instead of thirteen. When the instructions say you should move the aces to the foundation—that means all eight aces.

70. NAPOLEON AT ST. HELENA

History is a set of lies that people have agreed upon, wrote Napoleon himself. So whether you believe the following story or not is up to you. We'll report, and you can decide.

The legendary one-armed French ruler Napoleon Bonaparte, in his later years, was said to have been something of a solitaire fan. When the British finally defeated him, they exiled him to a tiny island called St. Helena. The Brits were so worried that he'd rise up against them that they put 2,000 soldiers on St. Helena, which is just sixty square miles. They also had two ships circling the island day and night to guard him. Napoleon never did escape, but according to some people he did pass some of his time in exile playing solitaire.

No one knows for sure which games he played or whether he actually played solitaire at all. But even so, there are lots of games named after him. *Napoleon At St. Helena* is one of the best.

In it, you have to build up the foundation in suit. This is quite a familiar-looking game, but it is played with two packs of cards.

Like most solitaire games, it can be played with one hand, so it is possible that Napoleon was a fan. (He only had one arm, remember.)

Game type: Strategy
Aim: Build all of the cards onto the foundation
One game takes about: 20 Minutes
Expect to win this game: Sometimes
Packs of cards: Two

Set Up

Deal ten columns, each containing four cards. In each column, overlap the cards so you can see them all.

How To Win

As the eight aces become available, move them to the foundation and build them up in suit to kings. You win the game when you've built all of the cards onto the foundation.

How To Play

The top card of each pile is available for play. So is the top card of the wastepile, when you have one. You can build either on the foundation or on the top card of any column in the base. When you're building on the base, build down in suit.

You can fill gaps in the base with any available card.

When you can't make any more moves—or you don't want to make any of the moves available—deal cards one by one from the stock onto the wastepile. Remember, the top card of the wastepile is always available.

Redeals

There are no redeals in this game.

Advice

☞ Focus on creating gaps—these will give you room to maneuver cards buried deep in the piles.

71. LUCAS

If you like *Napoleon at St. Helena* but you'd like to win more often, these next few games are for you. *Lucas* and *Maria* have all the main features of the original, but allow you to win most of the time.

Game type: Strategy
Aim: Build all of the cards onto the foundation
One game takes about: 20 Minutes
Expect to win this game: Usually
Packs of cards: Two

Play in exactly the same way as *Napoleon at St. Helena* except for two differences:

1. Before you start, place the eight aces in the foundation.

2. Set up the base with thirteen columns, three cards in each.

72. MARIA

Game type: Strategy
Aim: Build all of the cards onto the foundation
One game takes about: 20 Minutes
Expect to win this game: Usually
Packs of cards: Two

Play in exactly the same way as *Napoleon at St. Helena* except for two differences:

1. Set up the cards in nine columns with four cards in each.

2. When you're building in the base, build down in alternating colors.

73. LIMITED

Here is a variation of *Napoleon at St. Helena*. There are more columns to build on this game. This means you get more room to move cards around, more cards in play at any one time, and you're more likely to win.

Game type: Strategy
Aim: Build all of the cards onto the foundation
One game takes about: 20 Minutes
Expect to win this game: Often
Packs of cards: Two

Play in exactly the same way as *Napoleon at St. Helena* except for one difference: Set up the cards in twelve columns of three cards each, instead of ten columns of four.

74. INDIAN

Game type: Strategy
Aim: Build all of the cards onto the foundation
One game takes about: 20 Minutes
Expect to win this game: Usually
Packs of cards: Two

Play in exactly the same way as *Napoleon at St. Helena,* except for three differences:

1. For the base, deal ten columns with three cards in each.

2. In each column, deal the bottom two cards face down and the top two face up.

3. When you're building in the base, build down in sequence; you may put one card onto another of any suit *except its own.* For example, you could put 5♠ onto 6♥, 6♣, or 6♦, but *not* 6♠.

When you uncover a face-down card, turn it face up then treat it like any other card.

75. RANK AND FILE

This is *Napoleon at St. Helena* made harder.

Game type: Strategy
Aim: Build all of the cards onto the foundation
One game takes about: 20 Minutes
Expect to win this game: Sometimes
Packs of cards: Two

Play using the rules of *Napoleon at St. Helena* except for three differences:

1. In each pile, deal the bottom three cards face down and just the top one face up.

2. When you're building in the base, build down in alternating colors.

3. When you have a group of cards in sequence on the top of a pile, you may move them around as a single unit when you're moving them to another base pile. If you do this, keep them in sequence.

When you expose a face-down card, turn it face up then treat it like any other card.

76. CONGRESS

This game is simple but strategic. It's a building game, but the building you do on the base is just as important as the building you do on the foundation.

As you're dealing the stock, you should try to build the base columns carefully so that you can unload the cards to the foundation later on in the game. Also, choose carefully when to move cards from the base to the foundation. Don't create a gap in the base unless there is a card you want on top of the wastepile. Don't trap low cards underneath high cards of the same suit. Do have fun.

Game type: Strategy
Aim: Build all of the cards onto the foundation
One game takes about: 8 Minutes
Expect to win this game: Sometimes
Packs of cards: Two

Set Up

Deal two columns of four cards. These form the base. Between the two columns, leave a space for the foundation.

How To Win

Move the aces to the foundation and build them up in suit to kings. Remember, we're playing with two packs of cards, so there are eight aces.

How To Play

The top card of each column in the base is always available for play either onto the foundation or elsewhere on the base. When you're building on the base, build down regardless of suit onto the top card of any column. Each time you get a gap in the base, you must fill it straight away using the top card of the stock pile or wastepile.

Deal the stock, one card at a time, into the wastepile. The top card of the wastepile is always available for play.

Redeals

There are no redeals in this game.

Advice

☞ Don't make spaces in the base until you see a useful card on top of the wastepile. You have to fill gaps immediately from the wastepile, so whatever card is on the top at that point will move to the base. You don't want your base stuffed full of high cards.

☞ Useful cards for the base tend to be low cards, cards that will allow you to create more spaces, and cards that allow you to free up low cards that are trapped under higher ones.

77. CRAZY QUILT

Although *Crazy Quilt* is technically a strategy game, anyone who has played it will tell you that it's a lot of fun.

The wastepile plays a fairly big role here; it's where you try to build all the cards.

Game type: Strategy
Aim: Build all of the cards onto the foundation
One game takes about: 20 Minutes
Expect to win this game: Sometimes
Packs of cards: Two

Set Up

From the pack, take one ace and one king of each suit. Put these eight cards into a row, the foundation. Now, to form the "quilt," deal eight rows of eight cards. Imagine each card is one square of an eight-by-eight chessboard, and turn all the cards on the "black squares" sideways.

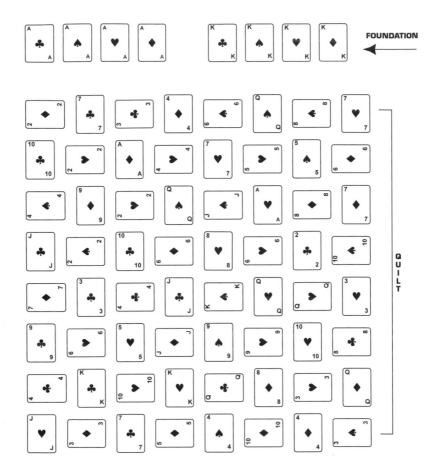

How To Win

In the foundation, build the aces up in suit to kings, and build the kings down in suit to aces.

How To Play

Deal the cards from the stock one at a time into the wastepile. The top card of the wastepile is always available for play onto the foundation. You may also build on the top card of the wastepile using available cards from the quilt. When building on the wastepile, build in suit either up or down—you choose. You may change direction as much as you like, building up, then down, down, up, down, and so forth, in any combination of ups and downs. You may build aces onto kings and twos, and conversely you can build kings and twos onto aces.

Now let's look at how to use the cards in the quilt.

Playing cards have four edges, two longer ones and two shorter ones. Those short edges are the ones you should focus on for this game. On the quilt, the only cards available for play are those with an exposed shorter edge. You can only move a card from the quilt if one or both of its shorter edges are exposed. That means a shorter edge must be next to an open space and not next to another card. So in our example, the available cards would be 7♣, 4♦, Q♠, 7♥, 6♦, 10♠, 8♣, 3♥, 4♦, 4♠, 7♣, J♥, 4♣, 7♦, 4♠, 2♦.

As you move cards away from the quilt, others will become exposed. In our example, we could move the Q♠ onto the K♠ in the foundation. This move would expose a narrow edge on the 6♠ and the 7♠ and make both these cards available for play.

Redeals

You're allowed one redeal. After you've dealt all of the cards from the stock, pick up the wastepile, turn it over, and it becomes the new stock. Deal the new stock one card at a time into a new wastepile and play as normal.

Advice

☞ Check to see whether there are any duplicate cards —both 6♦s, for example—buried in the quilt. If there are, try to release one of them as early as possible.

78. MAGIC CARPET

This variation of *Crazy Quilt* is more difficult than the original because at the start of the game all the cards are face down. That means you don't know which card is where.

Game type: Strategy
Aim: Build all of the cards onto the foundation
One game takes about: 15 Minutes
Expect to win this game: Sometimes
Packs of cards: Two

You should play in exactly the same way as *Crazy Quilt*, except for one difference. You deal all of the cards in the "quilt" *face down*. You may only turn a card face up when one of its narrow edges is exposed. As soon as a card is face up in the quilt, it is available for play.

79. SUPER CRAZY QUILT

You're going to need a lot of space for this variation of *Crazy Quilt*. You deal all of the cards into the "quilt." This means the game is fifty percent bigger than the original. It also means that there is no stock pile to deal. To help you when you get stuck, you're allowed to pick up a card from anywhere in the base. You're allowed three bonus picks during the game.

Game type: Strategy
Aim: Build all of the cards onto the foundation
One game takes about: 30 Minutes
Expect to win this game: Sometimes
Packs of cards: Two

You should place in exactly the same way as you'd play *Crazy Quilt*, except for a few changes. After you've taken your eight foundation cards out of the pack and set them up, deal *all* of the remaining cards into the quilt, which will comprise eight rows of twelve. There is no stock and no wastepile, but there are lots of exposed cards, which are available for play. As with the original, only the cards that have a shorter edge exposed are available. That's what we mean by exposed, in this game.

To start the game, choose any exposed card and place it in the wastepile. As with *Crazy Quilt*, you have to build all of the cards onto the wastepile regardless of suit. And as with the original, you may build up or down, switching direction as often as you like.

The main difference between this game and its predecessor is this: Here, you're allowed three bonus picks. What is a bonus pick? Well, if you get completely stuck, you're allowed to remove one card from anywhere in the quilt. The card you pick must fit onto one of the foundation piles, where you must build on it straight away. That is a bonus pick. You're allowed two further bonus picks: one on each of the next two times you get stuck. But if you get stuck for a fourth time, the game is over. Select your bonus picks carefully bearing in mind that you should use them to free up cards.

If you take your bonus-pick card from the middle of the quilt, you can start removing cards from around the gap left by that card. As long as a card has one or both of its shorter edges exposed, it is available for play.

Redeals

There are no redeals in this game.

80. VIRGINIA REEL

Everything changes. And the base of this game is no exception. Gradually it turns into the foundation and you aim to build the cards onto it.

There are quite a few rules to *Virginia Reel*, but once you've played it once or twice, you'll see that it's not a difficult game to understand.

Game type: Strategy
Aim: Build all of the cards onto the foundation
One game takes about: 18 Minutes
Expect to win this game: Often
Packs of cards: Two

Set Up

Take a 2, 3, and 4 out of the pack. Each of these cards should be of a different suit. So you might take 2♣, 3♥, and 4♠, for example. Place your three cards in a column to the left. Put the 2 at the top, the 3 beneath that, and the 4 at the bottom. This is the start of the foundation.

Next to each of these cards deal a row of seven cards, the base. You'll end up with three rows of eight cards, the left-most card of each row is a foundation card, and all the others are in the base.

Now, underneath the bottom row, deal another row with eight cards in it. This is the reserve. You'll end up with a four-by-eight grid. You should leave a gap to separate the reserve row from the base and another gap to separate the foundation. This helps you to see which cards are in which area.

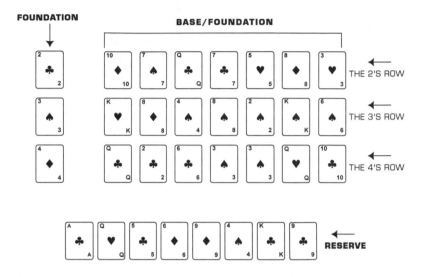

How To Play

This game is unusual because, as you play, the base gradually turns into the foundation. Read on and we'll explain how that works.

In the base, there is a row for the 2s, another for the 3s and one more for the 4s. These rows correspond to those first three foundation cards you laid out. The row next to the 2 is the row for 2s, the one next to the 3 is for 3s and the one by the 4 is for 4s. You'll also find the rows marked on the diagram.

When you can, move all the 2s, 3s and 4s into their own rows. As soon as a 2, 3 or 4 is in its own row, it becomes part of the foundation and you may start building on it. In just a moment we'll explain how to move cards. Right now, you need to know how to build on the foundation.

On each of the foundation cards, you build in suit. You also build up in threes, so follow these patterns:

On **2**s build in the following way: 2-5-8-J;
On **3**s: 3-6-9-Q; and
On **4**s: 4-7-10-K

You may use any card in the base or reserve for building onto the foundation or for turning into a foundation card. But when you move a card from the base, you must follow The Golden Rule for Moving Cards.

The Golden Rule for Moving Cards

On the base, you may only move a card away from The 2s Row if you can replace it with a 2 from the reserve or from another row on the base. If you replace the card using a 2 from elsewhere on the base, however, you must be able to replace *that* 2 with the card appropriate to the row it came from. So if you moved a card out of The 3s' Row you'd need to replace it with a 3, and if it were from The 4s' Row you'd replace it with a 4.

That rule is the key to this game—you may only move a card from the base if you can replace it with a card correct for its row.

Although you must stick to that rule, there are a couple of tricks that you can use to help you. The first trick is called the Double Switch. Look at the diagram: there is a 3♥ in the 2s' Row and a 2♠ in the 3s' Row. When you get a pair of cards like this—in each other's row—you may do a straight swap.

A similar rule applies when you have three cards in each other's rows. If you can move all three and end up with each in its correct row, you may make the switch. This is called the Triple Switch. Here's an example of how it works. Look at the diagram: there is 3♥ in The 2s' Row, 4♠ in the 3s' Row, and 2♣ in The 4s' Row. You can move the 2♣ to The 2s' Row, the 3♥ to The 3s' Row and the 4♠ to The 4s' Row.

That explains how to build and how to move cards. There is one more element of the game—dealing cards from the stock.

Deal cards from the stock in sets of eight, putting one on each of the eight reserve piles. The top card of the reserve is always available for play. While you are dealing those eight cards, you are not allowed to make any moves. But afterward, you should play as normal. You can deal a set of eight whenever you want to after you've set up the cards, but you aren't allowed any redeals.

In this game, you must discard all the aces. When you get an ace in the base, you discard it but you must follow The Golden Rule for Moving Cards. When you find that you've dealt an ace in the reserve, discard it as soon as you've finished dealing your eight cards.

You're not allowed to fill a gap in the reserve except when you deal a set of eight cards from the stock.

Redeals

There are no redeals in this game.

Advice

☞ Don't bury 2s, 3s and 4s in the reserve.

☞ Also in the reserve, look out for high cards covering other cards lower down in the same sequence, for example a 9 blocking a 6. Sometimes you'll be able to undo these tangles because, as you're playing with two packs, there are two of each card. Sometimes you'll be able to unravel them by building cards onto the foundation. And other times you won't be able to undo them at all.

☞ If you realize you are going to get stuck, you can challenge yourself to see how many cards you can get to the foundation. Keep a record of your personal best, and try to beat it.

81. WEST VIRGINIA REEL

This variation of *Virginia Reel* gives you much more flexibility and is easier to win.

Game type: Strategy
Aim: Build all of the cards onto the foundation
One game takes about: 15 Minutes
Expect to win this game: Usually
Packs of cards: Two

Play exactly the same as *Virginia Reel*, except build *regardless of suit* on the foundation.

82. DIPLOMAT

You should be able to win this game often, but that doesn't mean you don't have to think, and it doesn't mean that it isn't enjoyable to play. You do, and it is.

Game type: Strategy
Aim: Build all of the cards onto the foundation
One game takes about: 20 Minutes
Expect to win this game: Often
Packs of cards: Two

Set Up

Deal eight rows of four cards. In each column, overlap the cards so you can see all of them. As shown in the diagram, put four of the rows in a column to the left and four in a column to the right. Leave space for the foundation, which will go in the center of the arrangement.

How To Win

As they become available, move all the aces to the foundation and build them in suit up to kings.

How To Play

The top card of each row is available to build the foundation or the top card of another row in the base. When you're building on the base, build down regardless of suit.

Deal the cards from the stock, one by one, into the wastepile. The top of the wastepile is always available for play onto the foundation or base.

When you get a gap in the base, you may fill it with any available card.

Redeals

There are no redeals in this game.

Advice

☞ You should try to release low cards trapped under higher cards of the same suit. This isn't as much of a worry in this game. That's because you're playing with two decks, and there are two of each card, so even if one 3♦ is trapped under a K♦, there is still another 3♦ elsewhere. Nonetheless, you should take action if both 3♦s are trapped under higher diamonds.

83. WINDMILL

This is one of those solitaire games that looks like the thing it's named after. The cards are laid out in the shape of a windmill. Even if you're not well-versed in windmill design, you'll be right at home with this type of game, which involves building all of the cards onto the foundation using the reserve to help you. Unusually, you're allowed to transfer cards from some of the foundation piles to others.

Game type: Strategy
Aim: Build all of the cards onto the foundation
One game takes about: 8 Minutes
Expect to win this game: Sometimes
Packs of cards: Two

Set Up

Take any ace out of the pack and lay it down; this is the first card in the foundation. When you've done that, you should build eight reserves around it. Put two cards in each of the four reserves: two cards in a column above the ace, two in a column below, and a row of two to the left and another of two to the right. These reserves are like the sails of a windmill. When you've finished setting up the cards, you'll get an arrangement that looks like a plus sign (+).

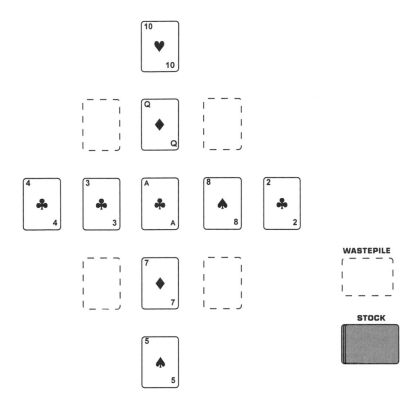

How To Win

To win, you must build all of the cards onto the foundation. You already have one foundation, the ace in the middle. Now you need to create four more using the first four kings that become available. As soon as a king is available for play, move it to one of the foundation spaces, shown in dotted lines on the diagram. Do the same thing with each of the first four kings that become available. Don't worry about the suits of these kings; it doesn't matter. Any suit will do.

As soon as a king is in place in one of these four foundation piles, you're allowed to start building on it. Build the kings down to aces regardless of suit. Each of these four piles should end up with thirteen cards in it.

On the ace in the middle, the other foundation pile, build up regardless of suit until it has 52 cards on it. Aces rank above kings and below 2s in this game, so when you've built your ace all the way up to king, you should lay another ace on top. Then on the ace, lay 2-3-4-5 and so on. This is called continuous ranking and it means that the sequence of cards forms a big loop—as soon as you reach a king, you place an ace on top of it and you keep working your way upward.

How To Play

The eight reserve cards are always available for play. So is the top card of the wastepile. When you remove a card from the reserve, you must fill the space immediately using the top card of the wastepile. If there aren't any cards in the wastepile, use a card from the stock instead.

You are allowed to move cards from the king-foundation piles to the ace-foundation pile. But you can only do so one card at a time. After you've moved a card from a king-foundation pile to the ace-foundation pile, the next card to go onto that ace-foundation must come from somewhere else, either the reserve or the wastepile.

Deal the stock one card at a time onto the wastepile. Remember that the top card of the wastepile is available for play onto the foundation or to fill a gap in the reserve.

Redeals

There are no redeals in this game.

Advice

☞ Build onto the center pile whenever you can.

☞ Don't create a gap in the reserve until you get a useful card on top of the wastepile.

☞ Try to keep a variety of cards in the reserve. Don't fill it with four 6s and four 5s. Have a range of ranks at all times. This makes it easier to build on that ever-hungry center foundation pile.

84. LORDS AND LADIES

In this game, different cards have different abilities. Some cards are "lords." They can be replaced from stock, and all of them are available for play all the time. Other cards are "ladies." Only the top lady of each column is available, and once a lady is moved, she can't be replaced. You have to use your lords and ladies to build all of the cards onto the foundation.

Game type: Strategy
Aim: Build all of the cards onto the foundation
One game takes about: 12 Minutes
Expect to win this game: Sometimes
Packs of cards: Two

Set Up

Deal two sets of cards. The right hand set, the "lords," contains four columns of four. And the left handset, the "ladies," contains four overlapping columns of three cards each. Leave a space for the foundation between the two sets.

How To Win

As they become available, move one ace and one 2 of each suit into the foundation. Build the aces and the 2s up in suit and in intervals of two.

On the aces the pattern will be: A-3-5-7-9-J-K-2-4-6-8-10-Q

And on the 2 it will be: 2-4-6-8-10-Q-A-3-5-7-9-J-K

How To Play

All lords are available for play all the time. Whenever you move a lord to the foundation, replace it straight away with the top card of the wastepile. If there isn't a wastepile, use the top card of the stock.

Only the top lady of each of the four columns is available for play. When you move a lady, you may not replace her.

You may only build onto the foundation and *not* onto another lord or lady.

If you get stuck or have made all the moves you want to, deal the stock, one card at a time, into the wastepile. The top card of this wastepile is always available for play.

Redeals

There are no redeals in this game.

Advice

☞ Before you do anything else, deal one card from the stock into the wastepile. This gives you one extra option for your first move.

☞ Only create a gap in the right-hand block when there is a useful card on top of the wastepile that you can fill it with.

☞ Move cards from the left-hand wing to the foundation whenever you can.

85. PALACE

This variation of *Lords and Ladies* gives you more control. You decide which cards have particular abilities and also which cards to start the foundation with.

Game type: Strategy
Aim: Build all of the cards onto the foundation
One game takes about: 10 Minutes
Expect to win this game: Sometimes
Packs of cards: Two

Play in exactly the same way as *Lords and Ladies* except for a few changes.

First, set up the game by dealing two sets of four rows, each containing four cards.

FIG 1.

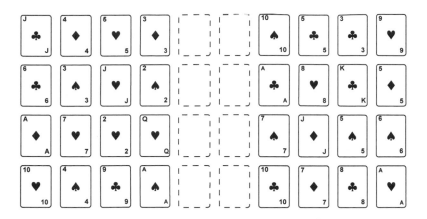

Take a look as both sets. As with *Lords and Ladies*, there are two types of cards. But in this game, you get to choose which set will be the lords and which will be the ladies.

When you have chosen which set will be your ladies, put the cards into overlapping columns, keeping the cards in the same order. Let's say that you chose the right-hand set as your ladies. (See Fig. 2)

FIG. 2

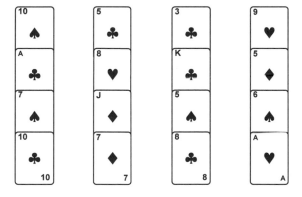

In *Lords and Ladies*, the starting foundation ranks are always aces and 2s. But in this game, you also have the power to determine what the two starting foundation ranks will be. So you might pick 6s and queens, for example, or maybe 8s and 8s. Whatever ranks you pick, you must move one of each suit to the foundation and build them up in suit and in intervals of two. Build up each of the eight foundation piles until they contain thirteen cards each.

86. INTELLIGENCE

A crucial part of this game is creating gaps. You have to create gaps on the base by clearing away entire columns because when you do that, you get to fill them from the stock. And that is the only way you can get the cards from the stock involved in the game. If you want to win, and presumably you do, you have to get those stock cards involved.

Aside from that, *Intelligence* has many elements of a classic building game. All the cards must end up on the foundation.

Game type: Strategy
Aim: Build all of the cards onto the foundation
One game takes about: 40 Minutes
Expect to win this game: Sometimes
Packs of cards: Two

Set Up

Deal nineteen fans of three cards each. Each time you deal an ace during the set up, move it to the foundation row and replace it with another card from the pack.

How To Win

As they become available, move all the aces to a foundation row and build them up in suit to kings.

How To Play

The top card of each fan is available either to build on the foundation or on the top card of another fan. Build on the fans either up or down, but always in suit.

Each time you create a gap in the base by moving all the cards out of a fan, fill that gap with a fan formed by three new cards from the stock. This is the only way you can fill a gap. It's also the only way you can get the cards from the stock into the game.

Whenever you deal an ace, during the set up or while playing the game, move it to the foundation and replace it with another card from the stock.

Redeals

You're allowed two redeals. When you get completely stuck and cannot make any more moves, collect up all of the cards in fans and the old stock, shuffle all of these cards together and redeal into nineteen fans of three cards each. Do not collect up the cards from the foundation. When you're redealing the cards, each time you deal an ace move it to the foundation and replace it with another card from the stock.

Advice

☞ On the base, try to create gaps as often as you can. This is the only way to get cards out of the stock and into play.

☞ If you realize that you won't win on a particular deal, it is worth forming unbreakable blockages on particular fans in order to free up cards to put on the foundation. All of the cards in the fans will be shuffled and re-dealt anyway, so it doesn't matter what state they're in immediately before a redeal.

87. GENIUS

Going from *Intelligence* to *Genius* is something like finding four quarters and then loosing a dollar bill, finding a tenner and loosing ten pound-coins, or finding one Gambian dalasi and loosing 100 bututs. How does this relate to solitaire, you wonder?

Well, in one way *Genius* is easier than *Intelligence*, and in another it's harder. You place the first eight cards into the foundation while you're setting up. This lets you start building sooner. But building itself is more tricky because you're building up on some cards and down on the others.

Which is better? Well, it depends whether you want to make a phone call or not. And which solitaire game is better? We'll leave that up to you to judge.

Game type: Strategy
Aim: Build all of the cards onto the foundation
One game takes about: 40 Minutes
Expect to win this game: Sometimes
Packs of cards: Two

Follow all the rules of *Intelligence*, except before you start playing take one king of each suit and one ace of each suit out of the pack and place them into the foundation.

You have to build the kings down in suit to aces, and build the aces up in suit to kings.

The top card of each foundation pile is available for play elsewhere on the foundation or onto the base. On the base, build either up or down on the top card of any fan. You may switch direction as much as you like on any particular fan. But you must always build in suit.

88. TOURNAMENT

A good solitaire game should be well balanced. It should be hard enough to be interesting but no so hard that it's confusing or frustrating. *Tournament* is an example of a game in perfect balance.

This game is a textbook case of building everything on the foundation. But there are a few things that make it a bit different. First, you're not allowed to shift cards round the base. The only place you can move them is directly to the foundation or to the reserve to fill gaps.

Filling gaps is the key to this game, it's how you keep things moving. You have to move cards from the reserve to the foundation to create gaps in the reserve. Also, you must create gaps in the base in order to release the cards from the stock. That's the only way that you can get to the stock cards. And you need to get all of the cards out of the stock in order to win the game.

So one card may be reincarnated four times in this game, starting as a lowly stock card, then moving up to the base, then to the reserve, and finally making it to the foundation.

Game type: Strategy
Aim: Build all of the cards onto the foundation
One game takes about: 15 Minutes
Expect to win this game: Often
Packs of cards: Two

Set Up

Deal two columns: four cards on the left and four on the right. For the game to work, you need at least one king or ace among these cards. So now you should check to see whether there is one. If there isn't, collect the cards up, shuffle, and deal again. Repeat this whole process until you get at least one king or ace. When you do, move on and deal the last part of the set up: Between the first two columns, deal six overlapping columns of four cards each.

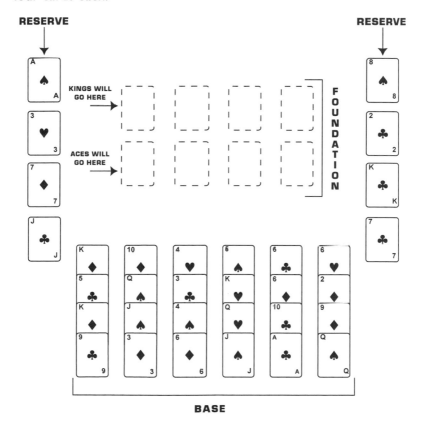

How To Win

As they become available, move one king and one ace of each suit to the foundation. Build the aces up in suit, and build the kings down in suit. If you get all of the cards onto the foundation —thirteen cards on each column—you win.

How To Play

All of the cards in the reserve are always available for play onto the foundation. You may fill gaps in the reserve using any available card from the base. You don't have to fill a gap straight away and may leave it open for as long as you want. In fact, as a general rule it's a good idea to keep at least one gap in the reserve at all times.

The top card of each base pile is available for play onto the foundation or into a space on the reserve. Unlike most other solitaire games, however, you cannot use it to build elsewhere on the base. So if you create a gap in the base by moving all of the cards away from one column, you must fill that gap immediately using four cards from the stock.

On the foundation, the top card of each pile is available for play elsewhere on the foundation and nowhere else. This is quite unusual for solitaire. In most games, once you put a card on the foundation, it must stay where it is.

When you've made all the moves you want to, deal four cards from the stock onto each of the six base piles. Now pause to make all the plays you want. Repeat this process of dealing and playing until you run out of cards.

Redeals

Redeals are always handy things. In this game you're allowed two of them. You should redeal when you don't have any more cards in the stock and you've made all the moves you can or want to.

When you're ready for a redeal, form a new stock pile by collecting up the cards in the base only—leave the reserve cards where they are.

You must collect the base cards in the following way. Pile up the cards in each column. Then place that new pile on the one to its own left. Keep going placing the new pile on its left-hand neighbor until you have just one pile. Don't shuffle the cards and make sure you keep them in the order you collected them.

Advice

☞ You should keep at least one space in the reserve throughout the whole game.

☞ Don't clog the reserve with cards that you won't be able to move until late in the game.

☞ When the two foundations of a particular suit meet, you find yourself in an excellent position. Let's say that you've built the A♣ up to 7♣ and you've built the K♣ down to 8♣. By shifting the cards from one pile to the other, you can get any club to be the top card. That means if you've got an awkward Q♣, 4♣, or any other card that is holding things up, you can just shift cards from one pile to the other and build the problem card on.

89. SLY FOX

There are a few things that spice up *Sly Fox* and make it more than just a run-of-the-mill game of building on foundation. The reserve is the main point of interest, and you are allowed a lot of flexibility in building up the reserve piles from the stock. You're also allowed to put any card onto any pile, so this gives you room to strategize to your heart's content.

Game type: Strategy
Aim: Build all of the cards onto the foundation
One game takes about: 12 Minutes
Expect to win this game: Usually
Packs of cards: Two

Set Up

Take one ace of each suit out of the pack; also remove one king of each suit. Place the four aces in a column to the left and the four kings in a column to the right. These two columns form the foundation. Now, between these two columns deal twenty cards—four rows of five. These are the reserve.

How To Win

To win, you must build all of the cards onto the foundation. You have to build aces up in suit to kings, and the kings down in suit to aces.

How To Play

There are three parts to this game. After you complete each one, move on to the next.

Part 1

To start with, all of the cards in the reserve are available for play onto the foundation. At this stage you should build onto the foundation. Each time you take a card from the reserve, fill the gap with a card from the stock. When you've made all the moves you can, or want to, fill all the gaps so there are twenty cards in the reserve and then move on to Part 2.

Part 2

At this stage, you may not build cards onto the foundation, only onto the reserve. Deal twenty cards, one at a time, from the stock; you may put these cards onto any of the twenty reserve piles. Which pile you put any card onto is up to you. You may put as many or as few cards as you want onto any of the reserve piles. Keep track of how many cards you've dealt from the stock, though, and when you reach twenty, move on to Part 3.

Part 3

The top card of each of the twenty piles is available for play onto the foundation again. Make all the plays you want to.

Repeat Parts 2 and 3 until you have dealt all the cards.

On your last deal, you'll probably have fewer than twenty cards in the stock to put on the reserve. If you do have fewer than twenty, when you deal your last card from the stock onto the reserve, move on to Part 3.

You are not allowed to move cards from one foundation pile to another.

Redeals

There are no redeals in this game.

Advice

☞ Your success will largely be decided by how you stack the cards on the reserve piles. Make sure you build some of the reserve piles up and some of them down. On an "up" pile, put higher cards on lower cards. And do the opposite on "down" piles.

☞ It is useful to build in suit on the reserve piles. But make sure that you don't build both duplicate cards into sequences going in the same direction. For example, if one of the 7♦ is in a sequence going up, the other must be in a sequence going down.

☞ Some players reserve a pile for the remaining kings and aces—these will be the last cards to go onto the foundation.

90. CRESCENT

Not only do you get a second chance, in this game, you get a third and fourth chance too. The bulk of the *Crescent* involves building on the base and foundation. But when you get stuck, you're allowed to bring cards from the bottom of their piles to the top. That will usually help you continue playing. You're allowed to do this three times.

Game type: Strategy
Aim: Build all of the cards onto the base
One game takes about: 25 Minutes
Expect to win this game: Usually
Packs of cards: Two

Set Up

First, you should form the foundation. Take from the pack a king and an ace of each suit. Now lay them out in two rows, kings in one and aces in the other. You should keep the cards of the same suit next to each other. To form the base, deal sixteen piles with six cards in each. Deal these piles face down in a crescent formation. When you have finished dealing, turn the top card of each pile face up.

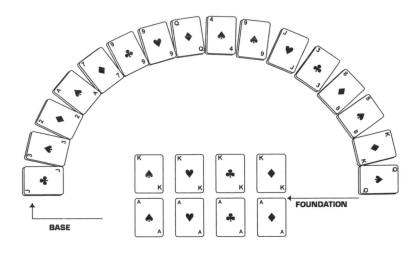

How To Win

In the foundation, build the aces up in suit to kings, and build the kings down in suit to aces.

How To Play

The top card of each pile is available for play, either onto the foundation or elsewhere on the base. When you are building on the base, you may build in suit—either up or down, as you want—on the top card of any other pile. And whether you're building on the base or the foundation, you may only move one card at a time.

When you uncover a face-down card, turn it face up. It then becomes available for play.

If you want to, you may also move one card at a time from one foundation pile to another. You can move any of the foundation cards in this way except the kings and aces at the bottoms of the piles—they have to stay put.

You're not allowed to fill gaps in the base.

When you can't make any more moves, you are allowed to perform The Shift.

The Shift

With every remaining pile in the base, move the bottom card to the top of the pile. If the bottom card is face down, simply turn it face up and put it on the top of its pile. You are allowed to do The Shift three times per game. If you get stuck after you've done your third Shift, the game is over.

Redeals

There are no redeals in this game.

Advice

☞ When the two foundations of a particular suit meet, you find yourself in an excellent position. Let's say that you've built the A♣ up to 7♣ and you've built the K♣ down to 8♣. By shifting the cards from one pile to the other, you can get any club to be the top card. That means if you've got an awkward Q♣, 4♣, or any other card that is holding things up, you can just shift cards from one pile to the other and build on the problem card.

☞ On the base, it is useful to build in suit.

☞ But make sure that you don't build both duplicate cards into sequences going in the same direction. For example, if one of the 7♦ is in a sequence going up—6♦ 7♦ 8♦—the other must be in a sequence going down 8♦ 7♦ 6♦.

91. SPIDER

We think this game is called *Spider* because you have to build the cards into eight long sets, similar to a spider's eight long legs. In any case, there is no foundation. So while you're aiming to build the cards into eight sets of thirteen, you do all your building on the base.

There is a handy little rule that helps you achieve this. When you have a group of cards built in suit and in sequence on the top of a pile, you may move some or all of those cards as one unit. You aren't stuck with moving just one card at a time.

This game involves lots of strategy. And if you're prepared to put in the thinking time, you should be able to win it quite often.

Game type: Strategy
Aim: Build all of the cards in sequence on the base
One game takes about: 25 Minutes
Expect to win this game: Often
Packs of cards: Two

Set Up

Deal fifty-four cards into ten piles. All of the cards should be face down. The first four piles on the left should have six cards each, and the other piles should all have five.

When you've dealt the cards, turn the top card of each pile face up.

You'll have fifty cards left over. These form the stock, which you'll use later on in the game.

How To Win

On any of the ten piles, build the cards into full sets of thirteen (K-Q-J-10-9-8-7-6-5-4-3-2-A). You should build the cards down and in suit. When you've assembled a set of thirteen, you may remove it straight away or later on in the game. It's up to you.

You win when you've discarded all of the cards in eight sets of thirteen.

How To Play

The top card of each pile is always available for play. You may build down, regardless of suit, on any other top card.

When you uncover a face-down card, you may turn it face up—it then becomes the new top card of the pile and is available for play.

If you have a group of cards that are of the same suit that are built down in sequence and are also on the top of their pile, you can move some or all of them as one unit. For example, if you have J♣ 10♣ 9♣ 8♣ on top of a pile, you can move all four cards as one unit. Because the bottom card of this unit is a jack, you can only build them on top of an available queen. Alternatively, you could move just the 9♣ 8♣ as one unit, in which case you'd have to build it onto a 10. You could also build 10♣ 9♣ 8♣ all together. Or you could just move the top card, 8♣, on its own.

You're allowed to fill gaps in the base with any available card or group of cards.

In this game, you can't build a king onto an ace. The only place you can move a king is into a gap.

Each time you get completely stuck, deal ten cards from the stock. Put one card face up on top of each pile. You'll have enough cards to do this five times.

Redeals

There are no redeals in this game.

Advice

☞ On the base, it is useful to build in suit. Do this when you can.

☞ But make sure that you don't build both duplicate cards into sequences going in the same direction. For example, if one of the 7♦ is in a sequence going up—6♦ 7♦ 8♦—the other must be in a sequence going down 8♦ 7♦ 6♦.

☞ Try to keep one pile to one suit and keep the building in one direction—up or down. It usually won't be possible to keep the pile to just one suit, but try to do this as far as possible.

92. MOUNT OLYMPUS

What's unusual about this game? Well, for one thing you set up the cards in the shape of a mountain peak, or upside-down "V" formation. Not unusual enough for you? Well, how about this? You do all your building in intervals of two. So, whether you're building on the base or the foundation, always remember to build in twos. Think like a cheerleader, and you'll be well on your way. Two, four, six, eight, who do we appreciate?

Game type: Strategy
Aim: Build all of the cards onto the foundation
One game takes about: 15 Minutes
Expect to win this game: Usually
Packs of cards: Two

Set Up

Take all of the aces and 2s out of the pack. Put the aces in one row and the 2s in another below it. These two rows form the foundation.

In a third row, the base, deal nine cards from the stock. It is traditional to form the cards into the shape of the mythical Mount Olympus itself. In case you haven't been to Olympus lately, an upside-down "V" shape will do nicely.

How To Win

To win, you must build five cards onto each ace, and six cards onto each 2. You have to build in suit using the following sequences:

On the **aces**: A-3-5-7-9-Q
On the **2**s: 2-4-6-8-10-J-K

You'll notice that you're building up in intervals of two.

How To Play

The nine cards in the base are always available for play. You can build them either onto the foundation or onto the top card of any other base pile. When building on the base, build down in suit and in intervals of two. You can, for example, put a 5♠ only on a 7♠.

Sometimes you'll create a gap by moving all of the cards away from one of the nine piles. When you do this, you must fill that gap straight away from the stock.

When you have a group of cards in sequence on the top of a pile, you may count that group as a single unit and move them together to another pile on the base.

After you've made all the moves you want to and have filled all the gaps, deal nine cards. Put one on each of the base piles.

Now continue playing: make your moves, fill your gaps, and deal nine more cards. Keep repeating this process until you have used up all of the cards in the stock.

Redeals

There are no redeals in this game.

Advice

☞ In each of the piles on the base, spread the cards so you can see all of them.

93. HOUSE IN THE WOODS

In this classic building game, the base is made of thirty-five fans. That gives you lots of places to build and therefore lots of flexibility. This is why, if you plan carefully, you should be able to win most of the time.

Game type: Strategy
Aim: Build all of the cards onto the foundation
One game takes about: 30 Minutes
Expect to win this game: Usually, if played carefully
Packs of cards: Two

Set Up

Deal out all of the cards into thirty-five fans. Thirty-four of them should contain three cards, and the thirty-fifth should contain two.

How To Win

As the aces become available, you should move them all to the foundation and build them up in suit up to kings.

How To Play

The top card of each fan is available for play onto the foundation or onto the top card of any other fan. When you're building on another fan, you may build up or down, but you must always build in suit. If you want to, you can build both up and down on the same fan, changing direction as many times as you want to.

You're not allowed to fill gaps. Neither may you build an ace onto a king, nor a king onto an ace.

Redeals

There are no redeals in this game.

Advice

☞ First of all, look at each of the fans. If any of them contain a lower card trapped under a higher one of the same suit, you should work to free the lower card. Then, when you are building up the foundation, try to build all of the piles at the same rate— try to get all of the 6s built before you move onto the 7s, for example.

94. HOUSE ON THE HILL

This variation of *House in the Woods* has a different feel. In the original game, you are always building up on the foundation, so you'll probably aim to build down on the fans as much as possible. But here, you need to build up and down on the foundation, so you'll need to do the same on the fans. That's why it takes more strategy to win *On the Hill* than it does *In the Woods*.

Game type: Strategy
Aim: Build all of the cards onto the foundation
One game takes about: 40 Minutes
Expect to win this game: Sometimes
Packs of cards: Two

Play in exactly the same way as *House in the Woods*, except instead of moving all the aces to the foundation, move just one ace of each suit along with one king of each suit. Build the aces up in suit to kings, and build the kings down in suit to aces.

95. ROOM WITH A VIEW

House in the Woods is pretty flexible, but this variation of it is even more so. You get more freedom when you're building on the fans. More freedom gives you more choices. More choices mean more opportunities to build on the foundation. More building on the foundation means more chance of winning more quickly.

Game type: Strategy
Aim: Build all of the cards onto the foundation
One game takes about: 30 Minutes

Expect to win this game: Usually
Packs of cards: Two

Follow all the rules of *House in the Woods*, except when building on the fans in the base, build up or down *regardless of suit*.

96. BIG BEN

You might like to think of the base piles of this game as a set of twelve bank accounts. You are supposed to keep a minimum balance of three cards in each. But because there are no penalties for going under this balance, you don't have to top up your "bank accounts," or foundation piles, straight away. If you decide to top one of them up, however, you have to top up all of them.

Aside from that, you aim to build all of your cards onto the foundation, which, like the base, is circular.

Game type: Strategy
Aim: Build all of the cards onto the foundation
One game takes about: 20 Minutes
Expect to win this game: Often
Packs of cards: Two

Set Up

Take the following twelve cards out of the pack:

2♣, 3♥, 4♠, 5♦, 6♣, 7♥, 8♠, 9♦, 10♣, J♥, Q♠, K♦

These cards form the foundation. You should lay them out in a circle and make each card correspond to one of the numbers on a clock face. First, put the 2♣ at "9 o'clock," then put the 3♥ at "10 o'clock," the 4♠ at "11 o'clock," and so on. Work clockwise putting one card at each "number." Keep the cards in the same order that they are written, above. You can check whether you've got the cards in the right places by looking at the diagram below.

When you've done that, deal twelve columns, each containing three cards. Overlap the columns so that you can see each of the cards, and arrange them in a larger circle outside the first. These columns form the base.

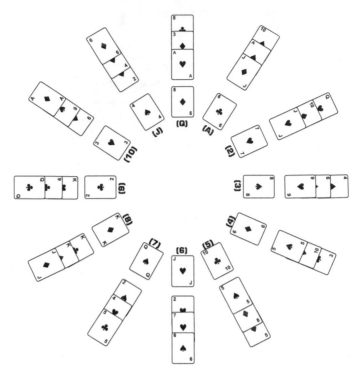

How To Win

Build each of the twelve foundation piles up in suit. The foundation is the inner circle, remember. Keep building until each pile shows the card marked next to it on the diagram. For example, build the 8♠ until there is a 3 on top of the pile, and build the 4♠ until it shows a jack. If you win, you'll end up with a completed clockface: a 2 in the 2 o'clock position, a 3 at "3 o'clock," and so forth.

How To Play

The top card of each of the base pile is available for play either onto the foundation or elsewhere on the base. When you're building on the base, build down in suit on the top card of any other pile.

When you're building, aces can follow kings and twos, and kings and twos can both follow aces.

Each pile in the base should contain a minimum of three cards. So any pile with fewer than three cards in it has gaps. If there are no cards in that pile there are three gaps; if there is one card in it, there are two gaps; and if there are two cards in it, there is one gap.

You must fill these gaps with cards from the stock, not from the wastepile or elsewhere on the base. But you don't have to fill the gaps right away. In fact, you can keep them open for as long as you want. But if you do keep a number of gaps open, you can't fill them one at a time. When you decide to fill one, you must fill them all, and you must do so in the following way. Start at "12 o'clock" and go clockwise around the base filling *all* gaps in the base—that means you must make sure every pile has at least three cards in it.

Deal the stock, one card at a time, into the wastepile. You can always use the top card of the wastepile for building onto the foundation or base. But you may never use it to fill gaps on the base.

Redeals

There are no redeals in this game.

Advice

☞ Scan the base for low cards trapped under higher ones of the same suit. Work to free the low cards where possible.

97. DICE

Here's another classic building game. You know the score by now: everything must go onto the foundation.

Game type: Strategy
Aim: Build all of the cards onto the foundation
One game takes about: 10 Minutes
Expect to win this game: Sometimes
Packs of cards: Two

Set up

Take the eight 2s out of the pack and set them up in two rows of four. This is the foundation. Next, deal a row of ten cards above the foundation. This is the base.

How To Win

Build the 2s up to aces in suit. In this game, ace is the highest-ranking card: 10-J-Q-K-A.

How To Play

Deal the cards from the stock, one by one, into the wastepile. The top card of the wastepile is always available for play either onto the foundation or onto the base. When you're building on the base, build down in suit. The top card of each of the base piles is also available for play either onto the foundation or elsewhere on the base.

If you create a gap by moving all of the cards away from one of the base piles, you must fill that gap straight away. To fill a gap you may use a card from the wastepile or the stock, but not from elsewhere on the base.

Redeals

You're allowed one redeal. When you've dealt all of the cards from the stock into the wastepile, pick up the wastepile, turn it over and it becomes your new stock. Deal the cards one by one into a new wastepile and play as normal.

Advice

☞ Scan the base for low cards trapped under higher ones of the same suit. Work to free the low cards where possible.

☞ Don't create a gap in the base until you get a useful card on top of the wastepile.

98. RED AND BLACK

As well as being enjoyable to play, this game looks nice. You have to build up the foundation in alternating colors—red, black, red, black—so you finish up with stripes.

Game type: Strategy
Aim: Build all of the cards onto the foundation
One game takes about: 10 Minutes
Expect to win this game: Usually
Packs of cards: Two

Set Up

Take the eight aces out of the pack and put them in a row. This row is the foundation. Underneath it, deal a row of eight cards to form the base. Later on in the game you will build these cards up to form base piles.

How To Win

Build the aces up in alternating colors to kings.

How To Play

The top card of each base pile is always available for play. You can move it onto the foundation or use it to build down in alternating colors on any other top card on the base. When you get a gap in the base, you must fill it straight away with the top card of the stock pile or the top card of the wastepile.

When you've made all the moves you want to, deal the stock, one card at a time, onto the wastepile. The top card of the wastepile is always available for play.

Redeals

There are no redeals in this game.

Advice

☞ Scan the base for low cards trapped under higher ones of the same suit. Work to free the low cards where possible.

99. DOWNING STREET

Each card must wait its turn. You have to move a king, queen, jack, 10, 9, 8, 7 and 6 to the foundation to build on them. But you must move them in order. There is no base to worry about. You just deal cards from the stock to the wastepile. When you deal a card that can go on the foundation, you move it there.

Game type: Fun
Aim: Build all of the cards onto the foundation
One game takes about: 8 Minutes
Expect to win this game: Often
Packs of cards: Two

Set Up

Take any king out of the pack and place it the left hand side of the table. This is the first card in the foundation row.

How To Play

Deal the cards one at a time into a wastepile.

As they become available, place any queen, jack, 10, 9, 8, 7, then 6 in a row next to the king. It doesn't matter which suit each of these cards is, but you must move them up in the correct order. You can't move the jack, for example, until the queen is already in place.

As soon as each of these cards is in place, you may start building on it. Build down regardless of suit until each pile contains thirteen cards.

How To Win

If you succeed in building all of the cards onto the foundation, you win the game.

Redeals

You are allowed two redeals. When there are no more cards in your stock pile, pick up the wastepile, turn it over and it becomes your new stock pile.

Advice

☞ *Downing Street* has the body of a strategy game and the soul of a fun game. There isn't too much strategy involved. Sometimes you may have to choose which foundation pile to build a card on.

☞ The general rule is to follow common sense and put it on the pile where it will give you the most moves afterward. For this reason it's useful if you can remember the order of the cards in the stock.

☞ Of course, we don't expect you to remember every card, but it's useful to have an idea of when cards are coming round, or if they've already been dealt.

CHAPTER VI
SOLITAIRE FOR
TWO PLAYERS

In this final chapter, we've included two-player solitaire games. Some people think that two-player solitaire is a contradiction in terms and that solitaire is, by definition, a game for one player. Other people think that the pattern of the game is the key thing, and if a two- or more player game follows most of the rules of a regular solitaire game, then, by golly, it is solitaire. We'll leave it to you to decide which side of the fence you're on.

We'll just say that the games are intensely fun and are based on the classic solitaire structure.

100. TEA FOR TWO

Tea for Two is a discarding game. But unlike any other in the book, it's is a game of speed. The quicker you are, the better you'll do. It's as simple as that. If your reflexes are faster than your opponents', you stand a better chance of winning.

Deal a base and a stock pile for each player. There are two wastepiles that either player can build onto, either up or down.

Game type: Fun, reflex, speed
Aim: Build all of your cards onto the wastepiles before your opponent does
One game takes about: 4 Minutes
Expect to win this game: Winning depends on the caliber your opponent
Packs of cards: One

Set Up

First, set up Player 1's base. Deal out fifteen face-down cards in five piles. In the first pile put one card; the second, two; the third, three; the fourth, four; and the fifth, five. When you've finished, turn the top card of each pile face up.

Now deal out five more piles in the same way for Player 2.

Finally, deal the remaining cards equally into two stock piles, one for each player. There should be eleven cards in each.

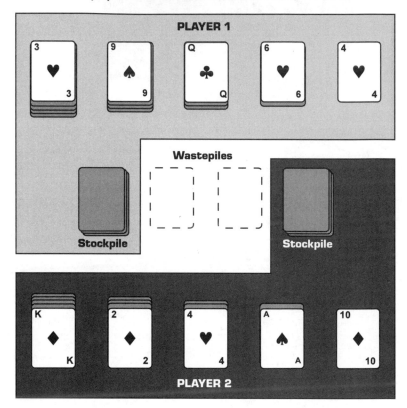

How To Win

You win the game by discarding all of the cards from your base before your opponent. And you discard cards by building them onto the wastepile. On the wastepile, you may build regardless of suit either up or down, changing direction as often as you like. For example, if the top card of the wastepile is a 7 you can build either a 6 or an 8 on top of it. If you put an 8 on it, then on top of that 8 could build either a 9 or another 7.

How To Play

Each player picks up the top card from his own stock pile and places it face up into the neighboring wastepile. Make sure you both do this at the same time. You'll get one new card on top of each wastepile.

As soon as the cards are in place in the wastepiles, you can both start building on the top card of the wastepile. The top card of each base pile is available for play onto the top card of either of the wastepiles. You can build either up or down, switching as often as you like, but you can only build one card at a time.

Aces rank above kings and below twos. So that means you may build aces onto kings or 2s, and you may build 2s and kings onto aces.

When you uncover a face-down card in your base, turn that card face up. It then becomes available for play.

You may fill gaps in your base with the top card of any other base pile.

You'll probably get to a point where both players can't make any more moves or don't want to make any of the moves that they can. When this happens, each player should deal one more card from his stock pile on top of the neighboring wastepile. Then you both continue building.

Repeat the process of turning up one card and then building until play is blocked. The player who gets rid of all his cards first wins.

Redeals

There are no redeals in this game.

Advice

☞ We advise you to remember that this is only a game. Sometimes your opponent will jump in ahead of you five times in a row. This can be frustrating, but don't take it out on the guy you're playing. The best way to avenge yourself is to pull the same trick on your opponent at the next opportunity.

101. DOUBLE TROUBLE

Twice as nice as *Tea for Two*, this game, we think, is something you will quite enjoy. It lasts longer, so there's more opportunity for exciting changes of fortune. Another nice thing about this game is that it's number 101 in a book that's only supposed to contain 100. This last game is a little bonus.

Game type: Fun, reflex, speed
Aim: Build all of your cards onto the wastepiles before your opponent does
One game takes about: 7 Minutes
Expect to win this game: Winning depends on the caliber of your opponent
Packs of cards: Two

You should play this in exactly the same way as *Tea for Two*, except you use two packs of cards and set up the cards in a different way.

Set Up

For Player 1's base, deal seven piles of face-down cards. In the first, you should put one card; in the second, put two; in the third, three; and so on. In the first pile, you should have seven cards. Now turn the top card of each pile face up.

Deal seven more piles in the same way for Player 2's base. Then deal the remaining cards equally into two piles. These form the two stock piles, one for each player. There should be twenty-four cards in each of these piles.

How To Play

This part is almost identical to *Tea for Two*. You have to turn up cards from stock and build like crazy.

The only difference is this: You are allowed to build on the top card of any base pile. You may build up or down, as you please, switching direction as often as you like.

How To Win

Get rid of all the cards from your base before your opponent gets rid of all his.

Redeals

There are no redeals in this game.

Advice

☞ Speed is key. A calm head and lightening-quick reactions are the best weapons.

GENERAL NOTES

A Word on Dealing

When a game's set up requires you to deal a number of piles, columns, or rows, there is a traditional way to do it. If you want to know what that is, read on.

To keep with convention, you should start by dealing one card to each pile, column or row (to keep things simple, we'll just say "pile" from now on). Then deal one more card to each pile. Each time you put one card on every pile, you've added a new layer. You should keep building all the piles up evenly, one layer at a time.

Let's look at an example. Say you have to deal six columns of six cards. First, you'd put one card into each column. Then you'd put a second card into each column. You keep adding layers until each of the columns contain six cards.

Some games, such as *Klondike*, ask you to set up columns of different sizes. The first column should contain one card, the second should have two, the third three, and so on.

You should deal this kind of set up in the following way. In your first layer of cards, you should deal one to each of the seven columns. Then, in the second layer, you won't need to deal to the first column—it only needs one card. So you skip Column 1, start with the next one dealing one card to Columns 2 through 7. For the third layer, deal one card to Columns 3 through 7. For the fourth layer, deal to 4 through 7, and so on. By the seventh and final layer, you'll deal just one card—to Column 7.

With *Klondike* and its kin, the top card of each column should be face up. The traditional way of achieving this is to deal the first card of each layer face up, and the other cards in the layer face down.

A Note on Some Alterations in the Games

This little section, tucked away at the back of the book, is for die-hard solitaire aficionados. You know who you are. And you may have noticed that some of the solitaire games are slightly different to the way you have seen them before. In *Intelligence*, for example, we've put nineteen fans in the set up instead of eighteen. We made these changes because we think they improve the games.

Like language, science, art, philosophy and most other things, solitaire is a constantly evolving, dynamic entity. In the process of writing this book, sometimes we found that a game was too hard, too easy, too short, or had some other limitation that meant it wasn't as good as it might have been. After experimentation, we found that adapting certain parts of certain games made them better. If we could make them one of the 100 best games in existence, we included them in this book.

Sometimes a game will have several versions, in which case we have picked the best and given it the name of the original. When there were several good versions, we've included them all.

Solitaire purists may complain that we are messing with tradition and that solitaire games have set rules. But this is not the case. The solitaire masters Morehead and Mott-Smith adapted and altered games as they saw fit. We are humbly attempting to follow in their footsteps by doing the same.

ILLUSTRATED GLOSSARY

THE BASICS

If you're used to playing with cards, you'll probably want to skip this section. But if you're new to cards, or you just want a quick refresher course, read on.

Base, Reserve—

Playing solitaire is like doing a jigsaw puzzle. The cards are like the pieces of the puzzle. You have to sort them out and put them together in the correct way to make the picture. Usually, the foundation is like the place where you put the pieces together. And the base and reserve are like the place where you sort the pieces out.

The base is also known as the *tableau*, but to keep things simple this book will always use the word *base*.

Color—

There are two colors in the pack of cards: red and black. Hearts and diamonds are red, spades and clubs are black.

Column—

A vertical line of cards.

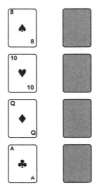

179

Continuous ranking—

Often the ace is both high and low—it acts like a link between the king and the 2.

This is called continuous ranking and means that the sequence of cards forms a big loop. King is followed by ace, which is followed by 2, 3, 4, and so on. Here is an example of a sequence using this type of ranking:

2-3-4-5-6-7-8-9-10-J-Q-K-A-2-3-4-5-6-7-8-9-10-J-Q-K-A-2-3-4, etc.

Deal—

To deal a card means take the top card from pack and place it down on the table, or whatever surface you're playing on. You'll usually deal a number of cards to set up the game. While you're playing, you might have to deal more cards, one at a time.

Face up and face down cards—

When you deal a card, you either put it face down or face up. If it's face up, you'll be able to see which card it is—the 5♣, for example, or the Q♠. But if it's face down you'll just see the pattern on the back of the card.

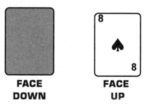

FACE
DOWN

FACE
UP

Fan—

A group of cards in a fan shape. The cards should all be touching at the bottom left-hand corner and spaced out at the top so that each card is visible.

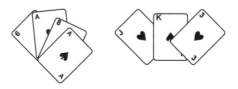

Foundation—

The foundation is the final destination for cards. If there is a foundation in the game, the aim will be to move all of the cards into it. You'll have to move them in a particular order, depending on which game you're playing.

Once you've moved a card to the foundation you're not allowed to move it again— it must stay put. But as soon as a card is in the foundation, you are allowed to build on it.

Overlapping column—

A vertical line of cards that overlap. You should be able to see each card in an overlapping column.

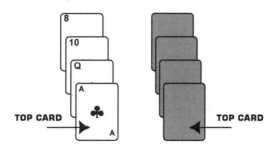

Overlapping row—

A horizontal line of cards that overlap. In an overlapping row, you should be able to see each of the cards.

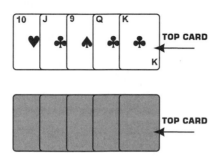

Pack of cards—

A pack of cards is a complete set of fifty-two cards. It is sometimes called a deck of cards.

You don't need the jokers for any of the games in this book. So take them out of the pack before you start playing.

For some of the games in this book you'll need one pack. And for others you'll need two.

Pile—

A stack of cards, one directly on top of the other.

Rank—

The rank is the number or picture of the card: 2, 3, 4, 5, 6, 7, 8, 10, jack, queen, king, ace.

Those last four cards—jack, queen, king, ace—are often shortened to their first letter of their name. So jack is J, queen is Q, king is K, and ace is A.

Row—

A horizontal line of cards.

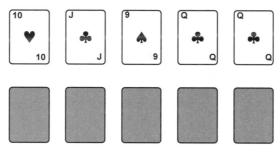

Sequence—

The cards in each suit have an order or sequence. The lowest card is usually 2. The next highest is 3, then 4, and so on, following numerical order. After 10 comes jack, queen, and king.

Low → → → High
(A)-2-3-4-5-6-7-8-9-10-J-Q-K-(A)

In some games the ace is high, ranking above the king. And in others it's low, ranking lower than the 2.

Shuffle—

When you shuffle the cards, you mix them all up so that they are in a completely different order to the one they were in before.

Suit—

Each card has a suit, a color and a rank. There are four different suits a card can be. Each of the suits has a name and a symbol: spades ♠; hearts ♥; clubs ♣; and diamonds ♦.

Stock pile—

To set up the game, you have to deal out a number of cards. After you've done this, you'll usually still have some cards left over. These are called the stock pile. Sometimes it's just called the stock. During the game you'll end up dealing these cards, often onto the base or **wastepile**.

Top card—

This is the card on the top of a pile, column, row or fan. You can tell it is the top card because it isn't covered by any other cards.

Usually the top card is the one that you can move or build other cards onto, so it's very important. The top card is marked on some of the diagrams below.

Wastepile—

This is where you put the cards that won't fit anywhere else. Sometimes you deal cards from the stock pile onto the wastepile to see if you can move them somewhere else. Not all games have a wastepile.

PLAYING THE GAME

Okay, you've familiarized yourself with the basics. Now you should read this section; it lists the words that you'll need to know to play solitaire.

HOW CARDS MOVE

As you've just seen, there are five places in a solitaire game. Not all games contain all of these five. But there are never more.

An important part of solitaire is how you can move cards from one place to another. Along with dealing cards from the stock, the main way you can move cards is by building with them.

Building—

Building is a key part of solitaire. It means placing one card on top of another in a particular order or pattern. There are a few different ways to build. You can build on the base, foundation, reserve or wastepile. And you can build in a number of different shapes: pile, row, column, fan.

Building can be compared to an ice cream: there are two parts to it. First, it comes in either a cup or a cone. And second, the ice cream has one of a number of flavors. The cup or cone part is like **building up** or **building down**. While the flavor is like building **regardless of suit**, **in suit**, **in color**, **in alternating color**, or some other way.

Sometimes you'll be able to build up and down on the same pile. This is pretty rare and, following the comparison, is like getting an ice-cream in a cup and then sticking a cone on top of it.

Building up—

Building up means you may put a card onto the next lower card. So you could put a 9 on an 8, or a jack on a 10.

Building down—

Conversely, if you're building down, you may put a card onto the next higher card. So you'd put a 6 on a 7, or a queen on a king.

Whenever you're building, you'll usually be building either up or down. But you will also build in another way at the same time. So you might build up in suit or build down in alternating colors.

Building regardless of suit—

This means you can build any suit onto any other suit. The only thing you have to do is make sure the sequence is right.

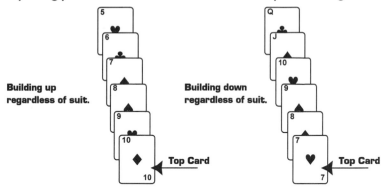

Building up regardless of suit.

Building down regardless of suit.

Building in suit—

When you're building this way, all the cards must be in the same suit. You can build either up in suit or down in suit. If you were building up in suit, you could put the 10♠ only on the 9♠. And if you were building down in suit, you could put it only on the J♠.

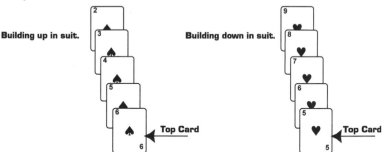

Building up in suit.

Building down in suit.

Building in alternating colors—

When you have to build in alternating colors, you may only put a black card on top of a red card, and a red on top of a black. You may never put one card on top of another of the same color. The red cards are ♥ and ♦, and the black are ♣ and ♠.

You'll end up with a striped set of cards: red-black-red-black-red-black.

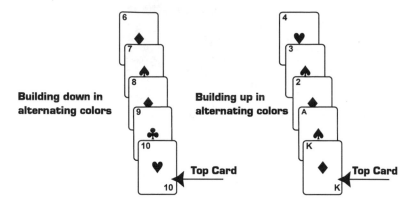

Building up and down on the same pile—

Sometimes you are allowed to build up and down on the same pile, column, row or fan. That means you may change directions as much as you like, sometimes building up and sometimes building down. When you build in this way, it will always be regardless of suit.

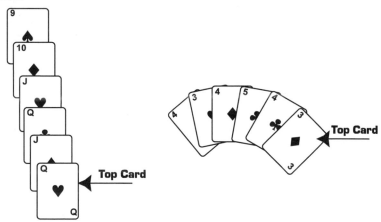

Other builds—

There are a few other ways to build—such as intervals of

two, or on any suit but the card's own. You'll only find these in a few games, so we'll explain them as they crop up.

OTHER THINGS TO DO WITH CARDS DURING THE GAME

In addition to dealing and building, there are a couple of other things you may need to do with your cards during the game.

Discarding—

When you discard a card you take it out of the game altogether. Once you've discarded a card, you can't bring it back. If you have to discard, it's usually because you win the game by getting rid of all your cards.

Freeing up—

You'll often find that a card you need is buried underneath other cards in the base or reserve. When this happens you'll need to shift cards around to uncover the buried card. This is called freeing up a card.

WHICH CARDS MOVE

Right, so now you know the five places of the solitaire game, how to move them either to build or to discard. Now you need to know which cards you are allowed to move.

Available Card, Available for Play—

An available card is one that you can lift up and move somewhere. If a card is **available for play**, that means the same thing as saying it is an available card. The top card of each pile is usually available.

Exposed Cards—

An exposed card is one with no other cards on top of it. It means almost the same thing as *top card*. So if you have a pile of cards and the top card is in play, once you move the top card, the one underneath is then exposed. It therefore becomes the new top card. When you expose a card, you remove all of the cards from on top of it.

SOME MORE USEFUL WORDS

Gaps—
Sometimes you'll clear away all of the cards in a pile, column, row, fan. This creates a gap. In some games you're allowed to fill gaps and in others you're not.

CREATING A GAP IN THE BASE

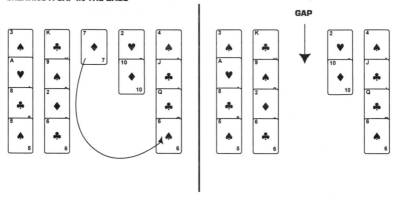

Getting stuck—
If you get stuck, it means that you can't make any more moves. When this happens, either the game will be over, or, if the game allows it, you'll be able to **redeal** the cards.

Redeal—
There are two times when you might be allowed a redeal. After you have dealt all the cards, or if you get completely stuck and can't make any more moves. Depending on the game, you may be allowed a few redeals, unlimited redeals, or none at all.

If you are allowed a redeal, you should collect up certain cards to form a new stock. Once you've done this, you get to deal it out and keep playing.

NOTES

NOTES

NOTES